T0294104

ONE IN A
MILLION

ONE IN A
MILLION
TREVOR FRANCIS

THE AUTOBIOGRAPHY
WITH KEITH DIXON

First published by Pitch Publishing, 2019

Pitch Publishing
A2 Yeoman Gate
Yeoman Way
Worthing
Sussex
BN13 3QZ
www.pitchpublishing.co.uk
info@pitchpublishing.co.uk

A CIP catalogue record is available for this book
from the British Library.

ISBN 978-1-78531-499-5

Typesetting and origination by Pitch Publishing

Printed and bound by TJ International Ltd,
Trecerus Industrial Estate, Padstow, Cornwall, PL28 8RW

Contents

DEDICATION

To my wife Helen

Acknowledgements

WRITING this book has been as difficult as it must be when a World Cup manager has to select his starting 11 from his squad of 23 top-quality international players.

My thanks go to my co-author Keith Dixon, who has spent time debating with me whether a story is worthy of inclusion or not. He has spent hours listening to my memories and stories and together we have decided how to present them in the right style for you, the reader. Keith has been the 'strong author' I requested. It would be fair to say that the content is mine, but the structure has been the responsibility of Keith. Together we have produced a book of which I am immensely proud.

Keith Dixon is the author of nine football books including *The Blues – Great Games Great Teams Great Players*, *Gil Merrick*, *Jackie Sewell*, *Birmingham City – 50 Greatest Matches*, *Birmingham City – Modern Day Heroes*, *Bad Blood*, *Robbo – Unsung Hero*, *Birmingham City – The Leaders* and *Blues Insider*. He was a regular contributor to the *Blues* magazine and currently contributes to the football magazine, *Late*

Tackle. Keith serves as a committee member for the Birmingham City Former Players' Association.

Thanks go to my family, my sons Matthew and James, my grandchildren and my brother and sister, Ian and Carolyn. I cannot thank you enough for your love and support. Roy and Phyllis, my departed parents, what would I have done without you? Thanks also go to Jane and Paul Camillin, Margaret Murray and Duncan Olner, and the team at Pitch Publishing, for turning my life memories into the book you have in your hands.

Introduction
by Keith Dixon

IT was Tuesday 6 March 2018 when I met Trevor to discuss my ideas for his book. Having spoken to him the previous Wednesday evening, I knew that he would need some convincing that we should write his autobiography. There was only one choice of subject for what would probably be my last book, and that was Trevor. I needed to persuade him that this project was worthwhile.

Trevor arrived dead on time for our meeting, stating that he hated being late. I share Trevor's dislike of being late so we were off to a good start.

We had worked together previously when he agreed to write one of the forewords (the other was written by Barry Fry) for my 2017 book, *Blues Insider*. Therefore, I was aware of his attention to detail and desire to get things absolutely right. During our two-hour meeting Trevor made it clear that he was only prepared to embark on this project if we both agreed that the end product would be top quality – in other words, the best book we could write. It was on that basis that we started this adventure.

I say adventure because, as a septuagenarian Bluenose, what greater accolade could I receive – in writing terms – than to write the life story of one of my Birmingham City heroes? In saying 'one of my', there are only two, the other being Gil Merrick whose autobiography *Gil Merrick* I wrote in 2009. In this way my first book and my latest are dedicated to the two most famous footballers to wear the royal blue of the Blues. Well, with Gil it was a green woollen jersey!

After discussion Trevor and I agreed that this new book should be fundamentally a football book, one that was exactly what he wanted, as long as I was happy with the potential content. He wanted me to act as a 'strong author' which meant ensuring the content was appropriate and relevant to the reader. With this in mind Trevor went off to consider what title he would prefer, fully aware that the final decision on the title of any book is the responsibility of the publisher.

He came back to me within a couple of days with the suggestion that the book should be called *One in a Million*. His thinking was based on the irrefutable fact that he will always be remembered as the first million-pound football player. I passed on the idea to the publishers and they agreed.

Trevor and I decided that the book would be encyclopaedic in terms of his career and that it would follow the traditional chronological approach. Trevor rejected my idea for him to voice his opinion on a whole range of footballing subjects as he felt that this would be inappropriate. After our first two sessions it became clear to me that Trevor had no interest in what other people in football thought of him, whether good, bad or indifferent. This meant that the research I had conducted and the many quotes I had obtained from his team-mates, as preparation for my proposal, were deleted from our initial draft.

What you have in your hands is a book that is full of personal recollections from Trevor's career. This is an intimate record of his life and career from his own very special perspective.

It has been a tremendous experience working with Trevor and listening to the stories, memories and anecdotes related to his life. Unlike some footballer biographies, this one does not pull any punches. It is 'warts and all' and names are named!

Enjoy the book.

Introduction
by Trevor Francis

THERE have been two books written about me to date: *Anatomy of a £1 million player* which was published in 1980 and *The World to Play For* which came out in 1982, so my story since then has never been told, until now.

I have an approach to life which I have applied to the writing of this book and it is quite simply, 'Do it right or don't do it at all!' I cannot see the point of taking on any project or task and being happy with second best. Whatever your opinion is, after you have finished reading my book please understand it is my absolute best effort.

Prior to my involvement with Keith on this book, I had been approached, on two previous occasions, about writing my autobiography. I rejected both offers because I wanted to make my book an honest testimony to my career and life. This meant that I had to write it after my involvement in football had ended so that I could tell it like it was.

There are very few statistics in my book. I believe that the detail behind many of the matches that I have been involved in as either a player or a manager is out there on the internet for those readers who want that amount of information.

Everything in this book is the truth from my personal experiences. There's no hearsay, nothing that was told to me in confidence. It's 100 per cent fact and some of those facts defy belief!

Too often I read autobiographies, sometimes about people that I know well, and I can tell that the person the book is about has not devoted much time to the published outcome. How do I know this? Because the details are not included.

How frustrating it must be for readers when a story ends with the statement, 'I am not prepared to name names.' So often this is the case, but not in this book. It is wrong that authors fail to justify their story with the facts, as it leaves the reader speculating about who it was and what actually happened. Although this means disappointment for the reader, it is not as bad as the absolute untruths that get printed. Let me give you an example: as part of our research we came across a book by Tom Bower entitled *Broken Dreams – Vanity, Greed and the Souring of British Football*. Tom has, according to the blurb in his book, 'a distinguished reputation as an investigative historian'. In the book he writes, 'The trade in Danish players was nevertheless curious … Krishie Pausen, bought by Trevor

Francis for Birmingham City for £5m, although worth, according to Scandinavian agents, at most £500k, who only played 12 First Division matches …'

As a reader you would take that at face value – the details are there, but are they accurate? The facts are these: firstly his name is Christian 'Kristie' Poulsen and, yes, he was a player I was interested in, to the extent that I watched him several times, both in his native Denmark (you got that right, Tom) and in the Olympic Stadium in Rome in a Champions League game.

That was it. Where did Tom get the so-called facts of a £5m fee and 12 appearances for Birmingham City?

For me the best stories are the true ones. I was keen to write this book because there are so many stories that will make the reader sit back in disbelief. But you have it from me it is truth.

Preface

IT'S 2019 and Trevor Francis is 65. On reaching normal retirement age it's the perfect time for him to reflect on his career.

Trevor Francis will always be known as the first player to command a transfer fee of £1m. The fact that it happened on two other occasions is rarely mentioned.

We have all seen players with exceptional pace, but what made Trevor special was his ability to run at pace with the ball coupled with the ability to know where to run and what to do with the ball when he got there.

The modern-day equivalent of Trevor is Kylian Mbappe of Paris Saint-Germain and France, who became a World Cup winner in 2018 at the age of 19.

Exceptional talent on its own is not sufficient, as there are plenty of examples of talented footballers who did not realise their full potential. Talent has to be accompanied by a passion for the game and an absolute desire to always be the best. Trevor Francis had it all – he was the complete package.

By harnessing his talent, passion and desire, he became a valuable asset for clubs across the globe, making over 500 appearances and scoring more than 150 goals in England and Scotland. He played in excess of 30 games in the United States, resulting in a goals-per-match ratio of one to one.

With two clubs in defence-minded Italy, he scored an average of one goal in every five games, and even his three games in Australia resulted in Trevor scoring two goals. Although known predominantly as a striker, Trevor's contribution as a provider should not be forgotten, although unfortunately he played in a time when assists were not recorded.

Overall he made over 600 club appearances and scored more than 230 goals: almost a goal in every two and a half games.

He also played over 50 times for England and has medals related to league promotions and cup victories as both a player and a manager.

His long career meant that he played in the formative years of the English Premier League. But he was restricted to only six appearances, dictated by his own managerial decisions, such was his integrity as player-manager of Sheffield Wednesday.

Now a successful property developer, he has enjoyed a lifetime 'partnership' with his wife, Helen, to whom this book is dedicated. Together they have raised two sons, Matthew and James.

Trevor is a man who never enjoyed a normal adolescence, due to early fame and fortune, but he never let 'having too much too soon' turn his head.

Fame comes in a number of ways, such as when 'Trevor Francis tracksuits' appeared in the lyrics of the theme tune for the closing credits of the *Only Fools and Horses* television programme and then 30 years later his name was featured in the Screwfix television advertisements linked to ITV's coverage of the 2018 World Cup.

Trevor has experienced everything a long-term football career can throw at a person, and he has come through it without succumbing to the temptations that accompany celebrity status. After reading this book, hopefully you will realise that, despite it all, Trevor is a decent bloke, respectful of all his previous employers and the talent that was bestowed upon him.

It is now time to reveal the stories of a football career that lasted 34 years.

Chapter One

It All Started In Plymouth

I WAS born at 41 Morley Place in Plymouth on 19 April 1954. My love of football began at a very early age, playing with my dad, Roy, who was a semi-professional footballer in Victoria Park and sometimes on the Plymouth Hoe. My school, Pennycross Primary, was located on our council estate, and by the time I was seven I was playing for the school team with boys at least two years older than me.

This trend continued throughout my schooldays and at the age of 11 I was selected for Plymouth Schools Under-13s and I continued to gain schoolboy representative recognition at Under-14 and Under-15 levels, always as an underage player.

My favourite lessons at school were, not surprisingly, PE and games and I remember being decent at cricket. Whilst I did not particularly enjoy my schooldays I was a trier and was well behaved, although academically average. I developed a love for music, thanks to being a teenager when both The Beatles and The Rolling Stones were at their peak. That love of music has stayed with me throughout my life. I was at the Public Secondary School when at the age of 15 I decided to leave full-time education rather than miss a year of football apprenticeship.

At the age of 14 in 1968 I was sent on a Football Association course at Bisham Abbey and my report at the end of the course stated: 'fairly skilful but needs speeding up' – well the experts can't get it right all the time!

Whether that criticism stuck in my mind, I do not know, but as soon as I was an apprentice at Birmingham City I took steps to improve my pace, as you will read later.

My mum and dad, both no longer with us, were very supportive parents, and as their eldest child they made it quite clear that no decision on my career would be made until I was 15, and that the decision as to which club I would join would be mine, and mine alone.

But I know my mum was highly delighted with my signing-on fee, which was a washing machine!

In the 1960s it was not easy to get recognised as a footballing talent when you were based in the far south-west. Plymouth has never been an easy place to get to by rail or road and this was before the M5 was built. Scouts from the big clubs had plenty of potential talent on their doorsteps so why would they bother to travel to Devon? In the final analysis my choice as to where I would develop my football career was between three clubs: Plymouth Argyle, Bristol City and Birmingham City.

I and a boy named Kevin Griffin, who played in the same team as me, were attracting attention from the local club scouts. I felt there was little to choose between us in terms of goalscoring but I thought I had the edge on him in terms of other aspects of the forward's role.

At the age of 14 I was invited to train with Plymouth Argyle on an informal basis. It was never a trial but it gave their manager at the time, Billy Bingham, the opportunity to see me at close quarters. Bristol City also offered Kevin and me the opportunity to spend a week with them, which we did. Those were the days of John Galley and Chris Garland, when the Robins were a force. Kevin ultimately signed for Bristol City.

Plymouth Argyle, as my local side, were obviously interested and approaches were made to my parents not only by Billy Bingham but also their chief scout Ellis Stuttard.

Billy Bingham wanted to sign me but, as we now know, that never happened because fate played its hand and I was off to Birmingham, initially to play a representative game for Plymouth Schools.

I was playing regularly for the Plymouth Schools team and we were performing well in the English Schools Trophy competition. We had to play Birmingham Schools in Bordesley Green East, which is less than two miles from St Andrew's, the home of Birmingham City.

Don Dorman, Blues' chief scout, immediately saw my potential – which was no surprise as he was there to see me score a hat-trick which resulted in him talking to my parents and me about an apprenticeship. I remember Don saying the thing that stuck in his mind was that I struck the ball beautifully, unlike 99 per cent of schoolboys.

My success with Plymouth Schools resulted in my selection for a representative South-West Schools side to play in a trial game against a South-East side. The objective was to create a South Schools team that would play a North side which would lead to the selection of a national schools team.

The game was played in St Albans in Hertfordshire but I had been feeling unwell prior to the game. I always wanted to play football so there was no way I was going to pull out. That decision had ramifications because I did not do myself justice in the game and I was not selected for any more Schools representative side games. Suddenly I had developed great reservations about my ability. Obviously I knew I had not impressed the selectors for the South of England side and also the scouts from Arsenal, Tottenham Hotspur, West Ham, Wolverhampton Wanderers and Chelsea who were reportedly at the game.

This was one of those significant moments that can happen in anyone's life. You suffer a setback and you have to make a major decision about your future. It was my way, as a 14-year-old, not to give up after any setback and that has been my attitude throughout my life.

I agreed to sign as an apprentice, and, knowing that Blues had taken their full quota of 15 apprentices, it was clear that this was a chance I could not squander. I was excited about the opportunity I had been given and knew that after my setback in that trial game I had to have a realistic ambition. I decided my ambition was to become a regular in the Birmingham City youth team.

I signed for Birmingham City and 13 months later I was nicknamed 'Superboy'.

Chapter Two

Birmingham City FC

In all senior competitions 328 appearances, two substitute appearances and 133 goals

WHEN I joined Blues in the summer of 1969, I was not over-confident but I was determined to succeed. I had my objective of consolidating myself in the youth team and nothing or nobody was going to stop me. This, to me, meant working harder than all of the others. During my schoolboy days it had been suggested I lacked pace, which seems odd now looking back as my pace has set me apart from other footballers throughout my career. However, at that time in my development I took the advice and I would come back to St Andrew's in the afternoon wearing my spikes and I just ran sprints over and over again. It was worth it.

As a young man I understandably missed home and because of the distance between Birmingham and Plymouth Don Dorman agreed a special arrangement for the two-year duration of my apprenticeship: I was allowed home every three weeks. So on a Saturday evening after a game (all first-team games' kick-off times were 3pm in those days) I would make the six-hour train journey back home. Thanks to Don I did not have to return to Birmingham until the following Thursday. Good as this was, the arrangement only lasted for 12 months because after that I was playing for the first team.

I had a successful first season scoring quite regularly in the youth team and hadn't had more than a handful of reserve games before I was given the opportunity by manager Freddie Goodwin to be a substitute at Cardiff City.

Throughout my career I was never 'precious' about what shirt number I was allocated, as long as it wasn't 12!

I came on at half-time for Johnny Vincent in a game which we lost 2-0. That was where it all started for me – my first career record, as I became, at the age of 16 years and 139 days, the youngest player to play for the Blues' first team.

Freddie obviously saw something in me. You have to remember that even though I was scoring often I was not fully mature. I was quite frail – just a boy playing in a man's world. Physically the opposing players were far stronger than me, as I was probably four years away from my full physical development. It was an incredible adventure that I absolutely relished. The nice thing about that time in my career was that it wasn't just about scoring goals, but also about my general all-round game. I know, when I look back, that I was often making mistakes, but that was part of it. At the age of 16 who would not make mistakes, whether you were a footballer or in some other career?

That meant as a kid I was able to try things, I had a ready-made excuse. The management, my team-mates and the fans accepted the fact that I was just a youngster learning the game, but what that attitude gave me was enormous confidence to experiment – I was trying things that at times were outrageous but they seemed to come off well on a regular basis.

My full debut was the following Saturday at home to Oxford United. I remember the game and I remember the goal, but thinking back I also remember the Atkinson brothers, Graham, a striker, and Ron, a determined defender/midfielder, were playing for Oxford. Ron, who has become a friend over the years, regularly tells people that he had me in his pocket that day, saying I only had one kick all match – mind you that was the goal! Typical Ron.

I started scoring fairly often but the game that stands out in most people's memories is when I got all the goals against Bolton to become the youngest player to score four goals in a senior league match.

It's surprising how vividly I can recall the goals I scored decades ago.

It was on 20 February 1971 at St Andrew's that the Blues' fans saw my first hat-trick. The first goal came after

16 minutes when Gordon Taylor knocked the ball down and I lobbed it over their goalkeeper. Three minutes later Phil Summerill played the ball to me from Gordon's corner and I volleyed in my second. Twelve minutes from time Bolton's goalkeeper spilled a shot from Phil and I scored from the rebound to complete my hat-trick. I didn't finish the game as I was substituted with five minutes to go, having headed home Dave Robinson's cross for my fourth. The applause I got from the crowd was incredible.

I was taken off because I had taken a heavy bang to my thigh and the following Tuesday night we had a Youth Cup game against Arsenal at Highbury.

I needed intensive treatment after the game plus I had to come in on the Sunday for further treatment, in the hope that I could get myself fit for the Arsenal game. I was declared fit for the game and of course there was a lot of focus on me after the Bolton result. I didn't play well at Highbury as, believe it or not, it was a more difficult game than the previous Saturday.

Bolton's manager, the legendary Nat Lofthouse, had been most complimentary, saying, 'He's obviously got a natural gift for scoring just like Jimmy Greaves. It's instinct – something you cannot give players. It hurt to see him score four goals against us but he deserved them, we gave him nothing. He looks to have a fantastic future, I only wish I could swap ages with him.'

After the game I was in the bath when the players came off the field and I remember asking, 'Did Keith

Bowker have any chances?' Keith had come on as my substitute and I don't know who answered, but he said, 'Yes, he had a couple of chances.' My thoughts were that whilst I was happy, of course, to have scored four goals, I couldn't help thinking that maybe I could have scored more if I had stayed on!

Although my four goals against Bolton sparked all the hype about 'Superboy' it was part of an amazing run of scoring which started on 6 February and ended on 13 March. In six consecutive games I had scored 11 goals out of a total of 16.

Off the pitch Blues got a huge financial boost. There was a surge of interest in the club due to my performances, leading to over 10,000 coming to watch me in a youth game! This was significant when you bear in mind that previous home attendances had on occasions reached a worrying low of around 13,000.

Things had happened quicker than anyone could have expected but I was still an apprentice. For the apprentices, the days at our training ground in Damson Lane were good days. Each apprentice had to do certain duties throughout the week and, even though I was in the first team, and even after scoring four goals against Bolton, the following Monday I was out with the rest of the apprentices with our brushes sweeping the terraces.

We had to clean the boots of the first-team players as part of our routine duties. I was so pleased to be cleaning Trevor Hockey's boots that I rang home to tell my parents that not only had I cleaned his boots but that Trevor Hockey had spoken to me that day. Even though I was in the first team, I still had to knock on the door before I could enter the first-team dressing room. I was given no privileges over the rest of the reserves and apprentices; we all had to knock first. I used to mop the dressing rooms, clean the baths, do the first team players' boots and loads and loads of other things – on Fridays, we took it in turns to clean the manager's car.

We had to be at Damson Lane before ten o'clock on weekdays, to set up the kit and get the boots ready for the players' arrival. To do that I had to jump on a bus from my digs down to St Andrew's, and then we would go by minibus to Elmdon, where Damson Lane was situated. During my time as an apprentice I had three digs, in Stechford, Bordesley Green East and Nechells – not the most salubrious of areas but we got looked after well.

Modern day young footballers are not asked to do the duties we undertook, which is a shame because it instilled discipline in me and provided a good grounding for the rest of my career.

It is fair to say that my teenage years weren't exactly the same as those of most teenagers. At the age of 16 I had become headline news in Birmingham because of what I was achieving on the football field. This meant that my photos were in all the papers and I was getting a lot of recognition and a lot of attention.

When I went into bars with the other apprentices, who, with respect to them, weren't as well known as me, there was often a problem. On several occasions, I was asked to leave because my presence did cause difficulties due to the rivalry in Birmingham between Blues and Aston Villa.

I remember being surrounded by well-wishers when some idiot threw a pint in my face, so I got whisked out of the back door quickly. Things like that meant that I had to be extra careful in where I chose to go and therefore my teenage years were different to those of most young men, because I was a professional footballer. Players like a drink, and I was no different, but I couldn't live the life of the other apprentices.

In my first FA Cup semi-final against Leeds in 1972 we were very much the underdogs but in the semi-final in 1975 against Fulham we were the favourites. We didn't play particularly well at Hillsborough but we drew 1-1 thanks to a goal from Joe Gallagher.

So it was on to a replay at Maine Road in Manchester four days later. We played so much better but lost in extra time to the last kick of the game when a gentleman by the name of John Mitchell scored. I and the 25,000 Bluenoses there will never forget his name. Why? Because that was my biggest disappointment as a footballer – no second thoughts needed.

Losing in that manner – a goal that was bundled over the line when he didn't know too much about it – was hard to take. We had done enough to win the game and we should have been in the final.

As it happened that was my last opportunity as a player to get to Wembley in an FA Cup final although I did get there as a manager. It was the manner in which we lost that made it such a huge disappointment.

For me the Leeds United side of the early 70s was the best club side I have played against. Don Revie was a manager who looked at every situation to gain an advantage over the opposition.

Blues went to Elland Road in 1972 and I recall Freddie Goodwin asking central defender Roger Hynd to go on to the pitch about an hour before the game kicked off and stride up and down to measure both halves.

Roger came back to report that one half was six yards shorter than the other.

How much an advantage it was to the home side to know this fact I cannot imagine, but obviously Revie thought it valuable.

Apparently Freddie reported it to the referee on the day who promised to report it to the Football League but we heard nothing further.

I wonder if the Elland Road pitch is still the same?

After I had been at the club for 18 months, we got promotion in 1972 to Division One. Having got there, it was bit of a struggle to stay there but we managed to survive for seven years. I was improving as a footballer and I'd got into the England Under-23 team after playing for two years in the England Youth team, which twice won the Little World Cup.

Why did I stay so long? Well, for me, it was never about the money but instead was always about performing to the best of my ability whether for club or country.

The impact on attendances was phenomenal, with 52,470 showing up to an FA Cup game against Huddersfield. In that promotion year, the away following for the deciding match against Orient was and still is the biggest away support I have ever seen. I have never seen anything quite like it on the motorway going down to East London. The crowd that day was over 30,000 and I am not exaggerating when I say that at least three-quarters of the Brisbane Road ground were Birmingham fans.

I remember arriving at St Andrew's at 1.45pm for an Easter Monday home game and you could just feel the buzz around the ground. There were people everywhere outside and, once we were inside, the ground was nearly a quarter full over an hour before kick-off. Just remarkable.

I think it was pretty well known around the Birmingham area that Kenny Burns and I never got on. We did not see eye to eye because we are totally different characters. In his autobiography, *No ifs or butts*, he says that he was very jealous of me. I can't disguise the fact that we were different but nevertheless I had a lot of respect for him as a footballer.

He was very versatile as a centre-forward and when I played up front with him I witnessed first-hand his great attributes. The negative side of Kenny on the field was his lack of mobility and his lack of desire to run. He openly admitted that he never enjoyed training because he had to run and Kenny *did not* like running! This meant I found the workload as a partner to Kenny very demanding. I was having to do more running than I should have needed to do simply because Kenny totally ignored the need to run and did not want to close defenders down. He was more than happy for me to cover for him.

Those attributes I mentioned earlier? His hold-up play for a centre-forward was top class, technically he was very good and he was a good finisher. But his biggest attribute was his ability to head the ball. He could head the ball as well as any player I've ever seen and he had this ability to hang in the air. He could have been a top centre-forward if he had had a greater desire to run. I could still play football now if I didn't have to run but it was something you had to do and Kenny never relished it.

Brian Clough and Peter Taylor bought him from Birmingham City as a centre-forward in July 1977 for £150,000 and converted him to a centre-half. It was a very, very shrewd decision, because Kenny became an even better footballer as a central defender, going on to play for Scotland on numerous occasions and meriting a Football Writers' Association Player of the Year award in the 1977/78 season – a magnificent achievement.

When I had the opportunity to go to Nottingham Forest many felt that I wouldn't go there because they were aware of my problems with Kenny and thought that I wouldn't entertain going to a club with Kenny on its books. I think that would have been incredibly unprofessional of me, as the reason I was leaving Birmingham City wasn't financial. It was purely because I wanted to play with better players in a better team with a great manager, to give me a chance of winning things. As we now know it proved to be a wise decision.

In the autumn of 1974 I was called up to my first England squad and it was widely tipped by London's Fleet Street journalists that I'd be making my debut. Unfortunately I sustained a career-threatening injury at Bramall Lane against Sheffield United which put me out of the game for a long period of time. All I remember was going to strike the ball and somebody appearing to tackle me from behind. All I knew was that I had this terrible pain at the back of my leg. It was a very unusual injury because when the tendon was torn the ends had split, so it was like stitching together the strands of a horse's tail.

Freddie Goodwin wanted to explore every aspect of treatment, which was the club's prerogative. The first diagnosis was in Birmingham and the second in Leeds where I saw someone Freddie knew. Then it was down to London to get another opinion before returning to Birmingham. This caused a delay in my treatment but I knew it was only to seek out second opinions before taking action, which often happens with footballing injuries. Often in modern day football injuries like that are discussed with the player and the player's agent, but in my day you looked up to your manager as a kind of a fatherly figure and that was exactly how I saw Freddie, who I looked upon for guidance.

He was good to me and when he was sacked I was quite upset about it, but after the initial disappointment had worn off after a day or two, I went over to his house in Tanworth-in-Arden and presented him with an engraved cigar box just to show him my gratitude for what he had done for me. I just wanted to show my appreciation.

Eventually, I overcame that injury, got myself fit and was available for my second semi-final in the FA Cup. I played four league games prior to the semi-final, scoring two goals. It was a relief to be back at my peak after such a difficult injury.

There seemed to be a longish period of speculation about me leaving the club, simply because I had made it known that I wanted to win things before I retired from the game.

It was more difficult to leave a football club in those days because everything favoured the club. Later, the Bosman ruling changed football forever, making it so different today.

A footballer now, with the help of his agent, can manufacture deals quite easily. It wasn't like that in my time, even when I left Birmingham City. When I think about it there were only two clubs who were prepared to pay a million pounds as it was a huge sum of money. I believe if the asking price had been anywhere near the previous record of £500,000 the majority of the teams in Division One would have wanted to sign me, but it was an enormous amount of money – things were very different in those days!

I spent my years at Birmingham City hoping that when I left the club I would never lose my affection and passion for Blues. I think that was borne out by my performances. Probably my best years for goals was from 1976 to 1978. I am often asked when did you start to feel unsettled? It was undoubtedly the day in February 1974 that Freddie Goodwin called me at home in Knowle and said he'd just sold Bob Latchford for £350,000. I was so disappointed to hear that, even though in Howard Kendall and Archie Styles we had two good players coming in.

Ultimately I benefitted greatly from Howard because he could see a pass – he was a very perceptive passer of the ball. I enjoyed my time with Howard behind me but I also enjoyed playing with Bob Latchford. He was a good player and we had a good understanding.

We were mates off the field and we did well together on the field. I could see what he was experiencing in his time at Everton – he went there and became a very big player. It reinforced in me the understanding that I had to continue to play well at Blues to get a move, and I never failed to show the required endeavour.

People often discuss which was my best season. Some say the first season, others our promotion season of 1971/72. Some say the 1977/78 season when I was an ever-present.

My first season included the most memorable two weeks of my time at St Andrew's, when I scored in consecutive weeks – two goals against Sheffield Wednesday, four against Bolton Wanderers and two against Swindon Town. Eight goals in three matches!

The next four games were something of an anticlimax as I only managed to score three goals. The last of those goals was against Cardiff City at home, a game that attracted a remarkable crowd of 49,000. However, for the whole season I scored 16 goals in 21 league appearances.

The Cardiff match was the most physical game I had experienced up until then. It was a battle and I was being fouled on a persistent basis. Eventually a scuffle took place and lots of players were involved in pushing and shoving. Things had calmed down and then in the distance we saw big Roger Hynd pounding down the field towards where the scuffle had taken place. When he arrived players from both sides told him that it was sorted and to leave it alone, to which Roger replied in his gruff Scottish accent, 'I have to do it, the crowd expect it of me!' Roger was a character.

A month before this game we were away at Swindon Town. Nowadays there are formal regimented warm-ups for all the players in the squad, organised by the fitness coach. This was not the case in the 70s.

Each player was responsible for his own warm-up and Roger used to go through a heading routine in the dressing room, as heading was a strong part of his game. Unfortunately the dressing room ceiling at the County

Ground was lower than normal and as Roger leapt to head a ball he put his head through it.

The reaction from the players was mixed. One or two laughed; one or two were concerned for Roger's well-being and the rest were heard to say, 'Do you think he's realised he has put his head through the ceiling?'

My second season from an individual point of view resulted in me not being able to sustain the previous season's goalscoring exploits. Having said that I scored 14 goals in 45 appearances in all competitions, but the real success was for the team, as we secured promotion to Division One away at Orient in the last match of the season.

The turning point of the season was probably in late October 1971 when Freddie Goodwin bought Bob Hatton from Carlisle United for £30,000. During his time as manager, securing Bob Hatton must have been Freddie's best signing ever. Has there ever been a better front three in the history of Birmingham City Football Club?

From my point of view my best season was 1977/78 when I again made 45 appearances in all competitions but this time I scored 27 goals. Undoubtedly staying fit for the whole season played a big part in my having such a good domestic season but also in gaining my first international cap for England under Don Revie.

It was not the best season from the club's point of view because the team had three managers: Willie Bell, Sir Alf Ramsey and Jim Smith.

I was voted into the Professional Footballers' Association (PFA) team of the season and came desperately close to winning the PFA Player of the Year award but was pipped at the post by Andy Gray.

My time at Birmingham City was most enjoyable. If I did have any extra pressure I didn't let it concern me; I am a football man through and through. I just enjoyed playing football and so I enjoyed my time at Birmingham City, especially the year that we got promotion. Although I am not a great one for looking back at statistics, I find it fascinating to note the increase in the crowds that season as the word got around that you could see this 16-year-old talent that Blues had unearthed.

Whilst I was at Blues I used to write a column in the football comic *Roy of the Rovers*. I shared the column with the Arsenal striker, Malcolm Macdonald. We appeared in alternate editions.

Of the six hat-tricks I scored in my English league career the most unusual was the one I scored against Arsenal on 18 January 1977. The game ended in a 3-3 draw and who scored the Arsenal goals? None other than Malcolm. Now two hat-tricks in one game caused a dilemma: who got to keep the match ball?

On that occasion I got to keep the memento because it was a home game. However, that was not the case in Italy. I scored three for Sampdoria against Udinese. Their brilliant Brazilian, Zico, also got a hat-trick and he got to keep the ball.

I was doing well, Blues were getting better as a footballing team and the crowds were getting bigger which was evidence that the team was giving the fans what they wanted. If you know St Andrew's then you do not need me to tell you that when the attendance is good it becomes a fortress and a place that other teams find intimidating. The atmosphere created was very special and it was such a wonderful feeling for me being a youngster. The fans used to sing my name and I could tell by their reactions that they wanted me to do well. I felt it was just a wonderful time for me to be there. Even to this day, not a day passes without someone wanting to talk to me about the 70s.

I don't think that, unless you were a Birmingham City supporter when I came on to the scene, anyone outside of Birmingham could have fully understood the relationship between a set of supporters and a single player. Blues fans tell me to this day that, regardless of the era in which they supported the club, there has never been a time to compare with the 70s. I am told that this is because the club won national recognition for its footballing achievements and had a star player.

The honours gained by Birmingham City have been limited, but it is a fact that the FA Cup Final teams of 1931 and 1956, the League Cup-winning teams of 1963 and 2011 and even the Leyland DAF and Auto Windscreens tournament victors never had a true star in their line-ups. Let me hasten to add that this is not my assessment of the past teams but what I am told by diehard Bluenoses.

The Newcastle fans were special in the way they supported their stars Alan Shearer and Kevin Keegan. Although that hero worship was similar, in my opinion it never compared with the adulation I received at Birmingham. I believe that that support was unique – the way that Blues supporters travelled in their thousands to see me play, the way they filled St Andrew's to express their feelings for me, an individual who was giving them something in football terms that had not been seen before. It was an extremely humbling experience to feel the 'love' they had for me. One of my close friends is Jeff Lynne of the Electric Light Orchestra and he often relates the tale that he would sit in the stands at St Andrew's shouting 'give it to the kid' – it was so special and not just in football terms.

Evidence of the incredible backing I had from the Blues fans was apparent against Blackpool on 4 April 1972. We had been awarded a free kick from at least 40 yards from the Tilton Road goal and close to the Kop.

As I 'spotted' the ball I was looking to clip it into a forward area for our two big central defenders, which was what they were expecting. Then I could hear the masses of fans in the Kop urging me to have a go at goal myself. 'Shoot' was the shout. They instilled such belief and confidence in me that I thought I might as well go for it.

I drilled the ball with such power and accuracy and I struck it so sweetly I could see it rising. And despite a despairing dive from the Blackpool goalkeeper John Burridge, the ball hit the back of the net.

It was the first goal scored with 10,000 assists!

At the time I took it all in my stride. For me it was just another game but now, when I look back at what I achieved, I am very appreciative.

Scoring four goals in one match as a 16-year-old professional footballer is a record that will never be beaten! Why? Because now you are still at school at that age.

My greatest attribute was my pace with or without the ball. Together with my close control and vision, my pace meant that I could trouble defenders almost at will. On occasions I was selfish but because of my age it didn't matter. The players I was playing alongside may have got a little exasperated with me at times, because I didn't drop the ball off a little earlier or I tried to beat three players when I should have passed. I know they gave me the benefit of the doubt on a number of occasions because they recognised the fact that I was just learning the game. Also, I was learning the game in front of huge crowds and making a real contribution to the team's performance, and that made the difference in my team-mates' eyes. Even Kenny recognised my value to the team, particularly as I was doing his running for him. Whilst he may have appreciated my work during games he made training thoroughly unpleasant.

In five-a-sides he could be quite aggressive, which is an understatement; he was quite ruthless with some of his challenges. He often tried to cut me in two with a tackle and he succeeded on a few occasions. He wouldn't think twice about it. As we've grown older together, he has told me that he admired the way I dealt with the vicious tackles that were all part of the game in those days. Knowing Kenny's sense of humour, he probably thinks his attitude to me in training was helpful to me on matchdays. For whatever reason, the primary target of his tackles was me.

Undoubtedly, Kenny had a vicious streak in him at Birmingham but he was not like that at Forest. How do I know? Because I trained with him and did not get the same treatment from him that I experienced at Birmingham's training ground.

Kenny could have been an even better player for Birmingham if he had been managed correctly, as on occasions his aggressive play was counter-productive to the team. This aspect of his play was never addressed by his Birmingham managers, Willie Bell and Sir Alf Ramsey. Willie, a fellow Scotsman, was in my opinion far too lenient with Kenny and Sir Alf never really understood him and ultimately was the one who sold him to Brian Clough. Basically, he was allowed to be a thug. A thug called Kenneth was how he was addressed by both Clough and Ramsey.

I always remember Bob Hatton being an underrated footballer. He was part of the three that were often talked about in Birmingham – Latchford, Hatton and Francis.

When I was a very impressionable young man at Blues, Bob said something to me that has always stuck in my mind, hence the reason I am relating it now. I have always had such a love for football and absolutely loved training, and therefore was amazed when Bob said to me, 'Do you know, if I could get the same money as I do playing football, working where I used to on the Hull trawlers, I'd go back immediately.'

The reason that statement was such a shock to me was because I thought that if he felt like that then there must be others in football who thought the same. At that time I believed that everyone was playing for the love of the game with money being secondary. To me it was never about the money, it was about playing the sport that I absolutely adored. I don't think it would be too different these days, though. I believe that there must be players out there who, if they could get what they earn now doing something else, would do it. Amazing!

Sir Alf Ramsey found my situation difficult to the extent that on one occasion he recommended I be sold. At the time Arsenal were openly courting me, speaking publicly about breaking the £500,000 transfer record. Ramsey described their behaviour as 'disgraceful and irresponsible'.

In January 1978, Leeds United offered a blank cheque for me four days before Blues went to Anfield and beat Liverpool 2-3, a game in which I scored the penalty winner.

I gave my opinion on the situation, for which Ramsey fined me, declaring, 'Francis has had his say, his wife has had her say, now I'm waiting for the dog.'

Sir Alf left St Andrew's in March 1978 and Jim Smith was appointed. The rest, as they say, is history, and appears later in the book.

Chapter Three

America

In the North American Soccer League:
33 appearances; 36 goals

I HAD two trips to the United States of America, in 1978 and 1979 during the close seasons for English football. The opportunity to play in America came at a time when soccer was becoming extremely popular in the States and I was fortunate to be a part of the successful invasion of star footballers.

Many in the English game thought that the close season was for recuperation from the previous season's exertions and to allow preparation for the forthcoming season. Many Football League managers frowned upon the idea of playing football all year round. Brian Clough was very much in that camp but Jim Smith wholly supported the American adventure.

When I first went to the United States I was an established England international with 12 caps. It was unusual to have a current international playing in the North American Soccer League (NASL), as most players from the UK and other parts of the world were coming to the end of their careers and this was an opportunity for them to earn good money.

At the time of my first trip I was feeling fed up at continuing to not win anything. I thought America was something different and the offers being made to me were fabulous.

Jim Smith, who became Blues manager in March 1978, instigated my American adventure as a reward for my loyalty in staying with Birmingham City throughout the 70s whilst my peer group left to join bigger clubs, earn more money and win things.

There were three American teams interested in securing my services: New England Tea Men based in Boston, Minnesota Kicks, and Detroit Express controlled by Jimmy Hill.

This was a chance to earn £100,000 in three months which was more than I was earning in a whole season in England. The deal was for three years and the contract was with Birmingham City, not me.

In those days the clubs ruled the player's career, unlike today when agents instigate moves on behalf of their clients. Here was an opportunity to make some money – well, that was how Jim saw it on my behalf. I have never been a money grabber, but at the same time I considered that if I could make some money playing football in the close season then why not?

Detroit's home ground was known as the Pontiac Silverdome. It had cost $56 million and had a seated capacity of over 80,000.

The pitch was an indoor AstroTurf surface which suited my game immensely. The problem was that every game seemed to be played on a different surface – one week it was grass, the next an external AstroTurf pitch. There were also many variations of synthetic pitches. It was a challenge which I relished and managed to overcome as my playing record confirms.

The attendance for my first home game was 13,000 and everything was built around me. It became obvious very quickly that Detroit were not paying me just to play football, as I was also expected to be the club's number one public relations man. Often I would have to get up at 4.30am to drive downtown to either a television or radio station for a two-minute interview.

One thing about playing in America is that every away game is a plane trip. We would always travel the day before a game but sometimes I would have to travel out a day earlier than the rest of the team, with the club's press officer, to conduct a press conference two days ahead of the game. It was all about getting the message out there.

Whilst no expense was spared in some areas, e.g. marketing, there was a complete lack of investment in other areas. The training facilities were poor and some of the pitches we played on were also marked out for baseball.

Having said that my favourite venue was the Astrodome in Houston, Texas.

I was allocated the shirt number 20 and given the nickname 'The Wizard'.

My team-mates were from across the world. Apart from the two compulsory US citizens they were from England, Canada, South Africa, Denmark, Germany, Argentina, Brazil, Yugoslavia and Haiti. A real United Nations.

American soccer was all about the razzamatazz: interactive scoreboards, the 'Girl-Guard of Honour', i.e. cheerleaders, Trevor Francis 'Wizardy' T-shirts which were sponsored by 7-Eleven Food Stores, and the countdown introductions as the players came into the stadium. Mine was, 'Nummer Twennee ... Trevor Fraan-cis!'

As the star player I was always last to be called out and I remember once lining up in the tunnel alongside Alan Ball and Johnny Giles who were playing for Philadelphia Fury. I got someone to go and get my autograph book and got both of them to sign it before we went out on the pitch. It was amazing to think that probably 90 per cent of the crowd had never heard of either of them. Other well-known Brits were George Best at Fort Lauderdale and Rodney Marsh at Tampa Bay Rowdies.

The attendance in my final game of that season was 30,000 so I feel that I had paid for myself by more than doubling the people interested in attending a Detroit Express soccer match.

I was chosen for the NASL All-Star team in both 1978 and 1979. The team included players such as Johan Cruyff and Giorgio Chinaglia. I was proud of this achievement because my rivals for the forward position included Gerd Muller and George Best!

Although the US Media created awards and recognitions for the players, my own personal memories are more important. In March 1979 I scored six goals in a friendly game against New York Cosmos. The final goal in that 8-2 victory was one of my most memorable. I ran with the ball from the centre circle, passed a couple of players and as I came to the 18-yard box a Cosmos played shouted, 'Shoot'. It was Franz Beckenbauer and I remember the look on his face when my right-foot shot hit the roof of the net.

Beckenbauer was a prodigious defender and footballer and it meant so much to me to have scored six goals against him.

I believe my record of averaging a goal in every game is still a record in NASL history. To be fair, my goalscoring exploits were helped by the 'blue line', which meant that a player could not be offside if he was more than 35 yards from his opponent's goal. This rule definitely suited my style of play.

My goals total was 25 including an NASL record five goals in a 10-0 win over San Jose Earthquakes in my first season.

My involvement in US soccer was guided by Jimmy Hill, who had built up Coventry City. At the time he was

Coventry chairman through his British-based company World Sports Academy, which had invested £250,000 as part of Detroit Express's NASL franchise costs.

For my second trip to America my salary increased from £100,000 to £125,000. Another of those myths that have surrounded my career was that Birmingham City received £30,000 for my loan period. This was not the case.

Having failed in his efforts to get me on a loan deal with Minnesota Kicks, Freddie Goodwin, who was now their manager, then tried to get me on a permanent deal offering £600,000, which was immediately rejected by Jim Smith.

So I was back off to the USA.

The American experience enabled me to show that money wasn't the be all and end all for me. I went to Detroit as a Birmingham City player, because of Jimmy Hill. I was paid £100,000, which was an enormous amount of money in those days, and the second year, as a Nottingham Forest player, it was to be £125,000 – but I never got paid.

When he was signing my contracts Jimmy would always make the point that contracts don't really matter because if he reneged on the deal I could just go to Fleet Street. Why go to Fleet Street? Simply because at the time Jimmy Hill was one of the biggest names in football and Fleet Street would have paid me a small fortune to expose him. I told him that he didn't know me very well, as it certainly wasn't my style to go running off to the press to get money. However, little did I know that ultimately I wasn't going to get paid.

At the time Jimmy was extremely high profile, presenting BBC Television's *Match of the Day* and coverage of England's internationals. After his failure to pay me he was, at times, a little critical of me on the television, which I thought was a bit rich considering what had happened between us.

Nevertheless, I realised it was part of his job so I let it go because I don't hold grudges.

I also realised that Jimmy Hill had invested a lot of money in the Middle East which he had ultimately lost – it was a financial disaster for him and even his associates told me he didn't have the money to pay me.

Some may say I was being a bit naïve but, whether I am naïve or not, if he could not pay me because he'd lost a lot of money, I actually felt a little sorry for him. If I had pursued him through the legal process then it would have cost me a lot of money with no guarantee of my getting the agreed £125,000. My approach worked and eventually he paid me £25,000 of the agreed fee.

These days there would be a claim for compensation for loss of earnings but that was never considered in 1979, which meant that I had effectively been playing for three months at my own expense.

I gave 100 per cent as always on the pitch but I have to say that the standard was not great. If I had to make comparisons I would say that if Detroit Express had been playing in the Football League in 1979 they would have been a Division Two team fighting relegation.

Training at Detroit Express finished on the Saturday morning in readiness for our match scheduled for early Sunday evening and in the normal course of events I went home to rest up prior to the game.

Throughout my career I have always tried to be very professional in how I prepared for any game. However, there was an occasion when I behaved in a terribly unprofessional fashion. This has been kept secret until now.

Along with one of my team-mates we drove my car to Detroit's Metro Airport instead of our homes. We went there to catch a flight to Cleveland which took around an hour. When we got to our destination we were met by a friend of both Jeff Lynne and Bev Bevan of the rock band the Electric Light Orchestra, who were playing an open-air concert that night.

We got to the band's hotel and spent some time with the lads before we went to the concert. As we were guests of the band we managed to get into the concert even though we did not have tickets. The venue was sold out so we both enjoyed the concert sitting on the mixer desk in the middle of the arena which held a crowd of 70,000.

The acts on the bill were Foreigner followed by Journey before the top-of-the-bill act came on stage. The show lasted four hours and it was a fabulous event.

We went back to the hotel for the after-show party which went on well into the early hours.

On the Sunday morning we flew back to Detroit with Jeff and Bev as they were keen to watch the game. We got back to my house and my wife Helen cooked scrambled egg on toast for us all before we all left for the match. Whilst it was not the ideal preparation for the game, I scored in a winning performance.

The inevitable happened as Jeff and Bev were spotted in the crowd and therefore had to go on to the pitch to be acknowledged by the supporters.

On this occasion no damage was done by my unprofessional behaviour but no manager would have been happy with my actions before a match. So many things could have had a negative effect on the game but luckily that was not the case.

Although there were always lots of youngsters playing soccer it has never taken off in the way many people thought it would. Why? I believe it will always be less popular than the traditional American sports such as baseball, American football and even basketball and ice hockey, just as American football is in the UK. There is interest but it is way behind interest in the traditional British sports, football, cricket and rugby. In my opinion the real reason why soccer has never taken off in the US as people expected is because the media has never got behind it due to journalists' lack of understanding of the game.

During my time there I remember that the rules of association football were part of the media welcome pack. They were having to write about a game they never really understood.

Helen and I enjoyed America, spending the summer of 1979 in a five-bedroom ranch-style house on the sunny side of Detroit and travelling around in, you've guessed it, a white Cadillac.

Because I wanted a better start to my second season at Forest, I went to Brian Clough and told him that I would cancel the third year of my contract with Detroit. He was pleased.

Chapter Four

Nottingham Forest FC

*In all senior competitions: 92 appearances and
one substitute appearance; 37 goals*

THE Birmingham City manager, Jim Smith, was insistent that if I was to leave the club then someone would have to pay £1 million. He made it clear to all clubs that he would not be changing his position on the fee. I am aware, now, that the level of the fee immediately prevented a lot of clubs, who would have been interested in securing my services, from making an offer.

Remember, it was double the previous transfer record fee of £500,000 which took David Mills from Middlesbrough to West Bromwich Albion and it had set the benchmark for future transfer fees. It was a lot of money, as transfer fees in those days were around £150,000 to £200,000. But to go from £500,000 to £1m within a month was something most clubs did not expect to happen. Why? Because £1m was an unprecedented figure and whether they wanted to or not most clubs simply could not compete at that level, as it was difficult to justify in financial terms.

There were only two clubs who were prepared to pay £1m. One was Coventry City and the other was Nottingham Forest. Speaking with Coventry, it became evident very quickly that the deal would be linked to the US opportunity in Detroit. Jimmy Hill, the chairman at Coventry and now the owner of Detroit Express, was very much at the forefront of negotiations and he made it very clear he wanted me at Highfield Road.

I spoke with Gordon Milne, Coventry's manager, and on behalf of the club he made me a very good financial offer, bigger than the one I ultimately accepted from Forest. But this was never about money – as long as I was getting a fair deal I was happy. I was pretty certain that, as it was a £1m deal the money would be right plus there was a 5 per cent signing-on fee.

Since February 1979 myth has surrounded the *actual* transfer figure paid by Forest and still does. There are two questions that I get regularly asked: What was it like playing for Clough? Was the fee really £999,999?

That second question is still asked of me and I guarantee that in the next few days someone will stop me and say, 'Clough didn't pay £1 million for you.' The myth was created by Clough himself. In his usual flippant way he knew that whatever he said would make headlines so he created the idea that a £1 million transfer fee might have a negative effect on me therefore he had reduced it by one pound! Not true – the figure was over £1,150,000 after the addition of the league's levy.

Birmingham gave me permission to speak with Brian Clough, so I took Helen with me and a colleague of mine who had assisted me with my pensions. He came along just to give me support in case there was anything raised that I was uncertain about. Don't forget, in those days there were no agents involved. It was a big day and I was understandably a little nervous. Whilst I can't remember the time of my appointment, I know Clough was late as he was over at Trent Bridge playing squash. When he eventually arrived he was still in his kit complete with racket. I subsequently found out that this type of 'strange' behaviour was part of his management style. Often things which he made seem spontaneous were stage-managed and rehearsed. Making a squash game that had overrun its time more important than a £1 million transfer was his way of putting things into perspective on behalf of the fans, the club and me. It was all pre-planned and of course it grabbed the headlines.

Helen and I were left alone in an office at the City Ground. It was all part of the plan of keeping me waiting and playing down the importance of the occasion.

It was something at which he was brilliant. Often in important matches including European Cup finals he would play things down – the bigger the occasion the more he played it down.

Eventually we spoke at length and I think he was a little surprised by how long the negotiations took. I'd written a number of things down that I wanted to ask him because my philosophy was not to renegotiate a contract. What I mean is that, when I was in club management, it would irritate me if a player, who had had a good season, wanted to immediately review their contract arrangements. As far as I was concerned once I had agreed a contract then I would honour that contract regardless and not expect any further discussions until that contract was due for renewal.

This being the case, it was important for me to be 100 per cent happy with what was being offered. Brian was very keen, as was Peter Taylor who came along to the meeting, for me not to leave that office until I had signed the contract. Whilst in contract negotiations I asked for a clause to be inserted in the contract such that if Brian Clough left Nottingham Forest then I could also leave the club. I was told by Brian Clough that this was not permitted by the Football Association and they knew this because Peter Shilton had asked for a similar clause to be inserted in his contract.

Clough wanted everything settled there and then. I said I was more than happy with what had been agreed. We had probably spoken for between three and four hours. To be totally honest I had more or less made up my mind to sign before we had sat down. Regardless of the money involved, this was an opportunity for me to play for Brian Clough and to play for Nottingham Forest, who were the only team, in my opinion, who could challenge Liverpool.

I was going there to play in a very good team with very good players, which could only help me become a better footballer. Helen never got involved in any of the football decisions but she knew I was of a mind to sign. I always asked her what she thought but in the end, she always supported what I wanted to do.

Their chairman was Stuart Dryden. I remember him popping his head around the door a number of times to see how we were doing. Clough responded, 'Chairman, when I've got something to tell you I'll let you know.' Dryden was a Justice of the Peace!

Clough commanded great power within Nottingham Forest, which in hindsight was critical for him to achieve what he did with a relatively medium-sized club. That ultimate power was part of his make-up and he would have wanted that same power if he'd become England manager, which was probably the reason the FA never considered him, despite him being the people's favourite.

I know I disappointed Brian and Peter by insisting that I went home to sleep on it and return to Nottingham the next day. I wasn't really going to sleep on it. The real reason I wanted to go home was so that I could telephone Gordon Milne. I wanted him to be the first to know that I wasn't signing for Coventry City.

Lots of press, TV and supporters were around the ground waiting for news, so they were disappointed as well.

This was not my first meeting with Clough, as we had previously been in contact at an awards event hosted by ATV. He was presenting me with the Midlands Player of the Year award. As I walked up on to the stage, he was saying what a fine player I was or something like that, but then he suddenly told me to take my hands out of my pockets and I replied, 'Yes sir.' It was like a schoolteacher talking to me. Was that stage-managed or rehearsed? You never knew with the Boss!

Whilst I was at the Blues, I was aware that Forest were on a long unbeaten run and I became intrigued by how long it could be maintained. In those days all matches kicked off at 3pm on Saturday afternoons, so by 5 o'clock all the results were known. We had a television in the dressing room at St Andrew's and it was always on after the game, announcing the results. I always wanted to know how Forest had got on.

It was the most incredible achievement not losing a game from 26 November 1977 to 9 December 1978. Forty-two Division One games in just over 12 months, and within a short time I was part of that incredible team.

At the end of my first season we finished second to Liverpool in Division One. These were heady heights for me after Birmingham City but for the final part of the season when it was evident that we would be runners-up it was a real anti-climax for my team-mates after being champions the previous season.

The following day after signing I made my debut. It was a wintry February and quite a few games had been called off including the first-team fixture. I had been out injured for a while and was short of match practice but I was fit. Clough said, 'We've got a game tomorrow down at the Parks in Nottingham against Notts County and you'll be playing for the A team.' So I did, in front of about 20 people.

I learnt after that a huge risk had been taken because I wasn't insured to play, because my player registration had not been completed which resulted in the club having to pay a £250 fine to the Football Association. I can't remember much about the game but I do remember the team talk at half-time when I was told that if you are going to play for Nottingham Forest FC you will wear shin pads – so I had to get some. Clough wasn't managing but he was on the sideline watching.

Surprisingly I didn't recognise Kenny when I first walked into the Forest dressing room, not because his features had changed but because he was a different person. In the period that he had been at Nottingham Forest and I had remained at Birmingham City he had become a totally different individual. Brian Clough had done an unbelievable job 'knocking him into shape' in terms of his personality rather than his football. He had also converted him into a top-class defender but I am talking more about Kenny Burns, the man, because as a human being he was totally changed.

We got on fine at Forest and never had a problem, even in five-a-sides at the training ground. I believe that was achieved by the strong management he had at the

City Ground in direct contrast to that he had experienced at Birmingham City.

Evidence of his new personality is apparent in how he has behaved towards me since the loss of Helen. Kenny has constantly called to see how I am, how I'm feeling, and he's been very supportive. I have to keep reminding myself: is this the same guy that I knew at Birmingham?

Kenny and I just got on with our careers. I never hold grudges so for me it was never going to be a problem when we first met at Nottingham.

There is no point in the holding of grudges. Even as a manager I never held grudges against anyone regardless of what they had done. Some would say that was a bit of a weakness in me, but that's the way I am.

I was so looking forward to, and excited about, going to Nottingham Forest where I was going to join a group that was very much united. That was down to the management – it was a very happy dressing room and in my experience a happy dressing room is more easily achieved when you're winning and we were winning!

My league debut was as a substitute at home to Bristol City with my full debut a week later away at Ipswich Town. Ipswich were a very good team, boasting the likes of Arnold Muhren, Kevin Beattie, Frans Thijssen, Terry Butcher, Mick Mills, Eric Gates, Alan Brazil and Paul Mariner. I remember being taunted by the home crowd from the start to the finish of the game with, 'What a waste of money.' It wasn't a game that people will remember – a turgid draw to be honest. I had very few chances but with less than ten minutes to go, a ball came in from the right from Martin O'Neill.

I went for it but couldn't get to it with either my head or my foot so I punched it into the back of the net.

The referee immediately penalised me. I knew it was wrong, obviously, but I was prepared to do that because I was so desperate to get off the mark and gain us a win.

When we went into the dressing room the Boss told us to sit down and as usual we listened in silence. He gave me the biggest bollocking I have ever had in football. He said, with a few expletives included, that it was bloody rubbish, it was *Roy of the Rovers* stuff and at Nottingham Forest we play the game correctly.

He went on to say that whilst I might have done that at Birmingham, which I hadn't, I must not do it at Forest. He finished by saying, 'Don't ever do that again! Get in the bath!' That was it, sharp and to the point, letting me know in no uncertain terms that he didn't do cheating. In simple terms that's what he was saying. I couldn't disagree with him so I had to be big enough to accept his criticism. Basically he didn't want to win by unfair means, a message which I applaud.

It wasn't the easiest of starts at the City Ground due to the fact that I had joined the club when it had just got through to the League Cup Final and the quarter-final of the European Cup, and I wasn't eligible to play in either competition. Not playing consistently in the first team was frustrating, making me feel like a bit-part player at the very start of my Forest career.

I was delighted to get my first goal at home to Bolton Wanderers and then to be at Wembley when we won the League Cup, beating Southampton 3-2.

Clough was a great believer that if there was a squad of players then we were all in it together – we were a group; we were united.

He also believed that those who weren't playing should feel part of it and to do that he would get them to help in the team's preparation.

Pouring the tea for the players was one method he used for uniting the squad. Both Peter Shilton and I were the high-profile players highlighted in the press as being asked to be 'tea boys' but it was not just us – everyone in the squad got involved. It was another example of how the Boss was clever in the way he manipulated the media, using them to great benefit.

He knew that telling the press that I made the tea would make a good story. What it was doing for him was showing that he was the Boss, and whether you cost 'sod all' – a free transfer – or you were the million-pound player didn't matter. The press ran away with the story, 'Million Pound Tea Boy' became the headline and it has stuck ever since. It doesn't bother me one iota because I was more than happy to pour one or two of the players a cup of tea, particularly if they were going to get us through to the next round of the European Cup. The Boss was big on team spirit, which is essential, because unless you've got it you can't win anything. Martin O'Neill and I took some of Clough's management techniques into our managerial appointments. We are both disciples of the Boss.

I would like to have a pound for every time I have been asked the question: 'What was it like to play for Brian Clough?' Football followers are so interested in Brian Clough that it seemed to be almost a fascination for them.

Whenever he was on television I would be glued to the box, as he made compelling viewing. You never knew what he was going to say next!

He commanded huge respect from his players. He had such a presence about him that he was the type of person, and there are not many of them, who could walk into a room and turn heads.

There was no real secret to his success. He had a reputation for managing by fear but that was far from the case. We feared letting him down but we never went on to that pitch feeling fear. We could never have played such attractive football if we had had fear in our bodies. Fear makes you tense and we were never tense!

With Brian it was never about individuals; it was always about the team. The shape of the team never changed – it was always 4-4-2.

All the teams in the club played the same way, which ensured continuity. If there was an injury to the first team left-back then the replacement was the second team left-back – it was as simple as that.

Everything Brian did was simple; nothing was complicated. What he was big on was control the ball, pass and move.

When I first went there I had the habit of flicking the ball to try and find my strike partner. He soon knocked that out of me, I'll never forget the number of times he used to holler, 'Trev, get a hold of the bloody ball!'

Our big centre-half Larry Lloyd gave me the nickname of 'Flicker' which he still uses whenever we meet.

We will always be remembered for the beautiful way we played the game but we should never forget how hard we worked to regain possession of the ball.

Because Brian was such a prolific striker in his playing days I felt that as a striker I was required to meet his high standards.

An example of his simplistic approach was apparent at corners and free kicks. At the beginning of a new season we practised techniques for those set pieces which he insisted we use throughout the season without deviation. For example:

- For corners, the kicker would strike the ball towards the near post for a flick-on. If the opportunity arose to take a short corner that was also permitted.

- For a free kick on the edge of the box, one player would touch it to a colleague to strike at goal.

Another strength was his man-management skills. He never missed anything during the course of the 90 minutes. He was big on rest and often you would come into the ground and train for no longer than 45 minutes and then you would be given two days' rest.

There was never any chance of players 'leaving it all' on the training ground. It was all about matchdays.

As a team we defended deep with a good goalkeeper and two centre-halves whose main requisite was to be able to head the ball well. Brian did not like central defenders dwelling in position and liked the ball to be played forward. During one game Kenny Burns passed the ball square across his own penalty box. Immediately Clough instructed someone to go into the office to tell his secretary to write a letter for Kenny. At half-time Kenny received the letter which was a fine for passing the ball across the penalty area! It was not about the size of the fine, it was just making the point – don't do it again.

We had a full-back called Frank Gray whose biggest qualities were getting on the ball, being a good passer and dribbler, joining in well and beating players. He could go all the way, link with John Robertson and get himself inside the box, but defensively he was not the best. In fairness he wasn't bought for his defensive qualities. I always remember one home game when Frank was a little subdued and therefore didn't really venture forward much. At half-time Clough said to him, 'Frank, get yourself into a forward area, get yourself in the box, get a shot in or win a penalty otherwise get in the fucking bath.' You can't be more to the point than that, can you?

As a management partnership there was none better than Brian Clough and Peter Taylor. Taylor was often responsible for many of the signings. He would spend time watching players on numerous occasions, often paying to go into the grounds unannounced so as not to alert the relevant clubs.

Whilst it was a great partnership, all the players knew there was only one boss and that was Clough.

On occasions during the season Brian liked to take himself off to his favourite holiday retreat in Majorca.

If proof was ever needed as to who was number one it was emphasised in the League Cup fourth round match away at Watford in 1980.

As players we were aware that the Boss had gone away. What we were not so sure about was whether he would be in the dressing room when we arrived at Vicarage Road.

When Peter announced the team and confirmed that Brian was not there, you could visibly see the players start to relax and lose a little bit of focus.

There was an intensity when the Boss was there, which was never quite the case when Peter was in charge.

That was very evident in what was to follow – a sub-standard performance which resulted in a surprise 1-4 defeat and exit from a tournament in which we had reached the final the previous year.

We had progressed through to the final of the European Cup, which meant a huge decision needed to be taken by the Boss because, due to some strange ruling, I was eligible for the final.

For the European Cup Final I was rooming with John McGovern, who was the captain and had played under Clough at Hartlepool, Derby and Leeds. They were close. I remember asking him whether he knew the team for the match. He said he had no idea and I believed him but if he didn't know the team then nobody did except for Taylor and Clough.

We had dinner on the Tuesday night over in Munich after which Clough said there would be a meeting. Understandably we all assumed that this would be the time when he was going to reveal the team. We all sat down and the Boss and Peter were at their humorous best. As a partnership they were terrific and had obviously talked about what they were going to say to us. It was all part of the plan to relax us the night before the game; the last thing they wanted was for us to get uptight.

To prevent that they called over the wine waiter and ordered a few bottles of Liebfraumilch and we all had a couple of glasses. In fact, one or two of the lads had more than a couple of glasses and were the worse for wear the following morning – the day of the final!

We went to bed still not knowing what the team was and Clough told us to meet downstairs first thing in the morning. There would be no training but he wanted to go on the coach down to the Olympic Stadium to have a look around.

Around 11 o'clock on the morning of the match he sat us down on the perimeter of the running track. There were a couple of injury doubts, one being Martin O'Neill and the other Archie Gemmill.

He asked how Martin was and he assured Clough that he had been training and was feeling fine. He then asked Archie how he was and he also said that he was feeling good, to which Clough responded by saying that was good news as both O'Neill and Gemmill were on the bench!

He then proceeded to name the team: Peter Shilton – Viv Anderson – Larry Lloyd – Kenny Burns – Frank Clark – Trevor Francis – John McGovern – Ian Bowyer – John Robertson – Tony Woodcock and Garry Birtles.

The look on Martin and Archie's faces meant they didn't have to say anything; their look told the whole story. Their disappointment was immense. But for me? How fortunate was I to be making my debut in European football in the final?

Later we came downstairs and had a bit of a pre-match chat as we were all quite keen to get off to the stadium. Oblivious to what we wanted, the Boss sat us down outside in a small area of tables and chairs. Garry Birtles was the last to come down and it was obvious that he had not shaved for at least two days and was sprouting a beard. Clough told him in no uncertain terms to get back up to his room and shave, otherwise he was not playing! Even though we were already a little bit tight for time, we had to wait for him. We arrived at the stadium much later than any of us would have wanted, but it was all done for a reason: so that we didn't get there too early and potentially get carried away with the occasion. It was a big occasion, a huge occasion, we had huge support, so it was yet another example of the Boss playing things down.

Personally I felt added pressure because I recognised how fortunate I was to be playing. I really felt that I had to justify my inclusion with a top performance, to repay the Boss's decision. Having said that my selection was not a great surprise to me. I was always confident that I would be playing, and I think most of the other players shared that thought. When you think about it, it was a one-off match and you had a million-pound player available who could be a match-winner – why wouldn't you play him?

I know Martin O'Neill would put up a very strong case as to why he believes he should have played. I know that to be the case because all of the European Cup-winning squad keep in touch with one another, and Martin's become one of my biggest friends. Whenever we are together he rarely misses the opportunity to mention it. Little did he know that he'd get his chance to win the European Cup 12 months later!

At pre-match we just talked about ourselves as usual; we didn't mention the opposition. We knew what we had to do, we knew the roles we had to play, we knew about the expectations.

It wasn't a particularly exciting final but we won the game. Malmo were a very well-drilled side under English manager Bob Houghton, which resulted in them constantly catching us offside.

I was always told by Clough that whenever John Robertson had possession I had to make sure that I got in at the back post, because rarely did he not go past the full-back and deliver a cross.

With half-time approaching I remember the ball was played out to a wide area by Ian Bowyer. I was in a very deep position, a long way from goal, so I had to start motoring. As soon as John had the ball under control he beat two Swedish defenders and I knew that I had to get inside that box as soon as possible, so I had to make up a lot of ground to make sure I was there at that back post. I did not want to face the anger of the Boss by not being there! John whipped in a cross that their goalkeeper, Moller, could not get near. I got there and put us in the lead just on half-time, which probably changed the half-time team talk.

It transpired that it was the only goal of the game, not the best goal I have ever scored but undoubtedly the most important.

I was happy with my overall performance bearing in mind that I wasn't in my preferred position. It was a position that didn't come naturally to me, playing wide right. Remember, for nine years I had played top-level football as a striker, therefore I understood that position. I knew my role as a striker.

Playing on the right I was thinking throughout the game about what and where my position should be especially when we were out of possession. We were a good side in possession but probably an even better side when we didn't have the ball.

At the time, John was given the acclaim that he merited and we all recognised his importance, none more so than the Boss. 'Robbo' was up there amongst the very best in Europe. He could use both feet comfortably and he was very, very quick over five yards. He had the ability to drop his shoulder and go past players. Often, because of this, he would bring another player over to him, leaving gaps in the opposition defence. He used his two-footed skill to go inside and still deliver. He was a great crosser of the ball and he played with his head up, which meant he had great vision. Two players would come to him and he would get the ball on his right foot and just play it into the feet of the front man. He had that ability. If you think about his goal in the 1980 European Cup Final he came inside on to his right, played it in to Birtles, followed his pass and as Birtles held off the defender he passed it back to John who had one touch and scored.

Against Malmo, John wouldn't have picked me out. He just delivered the ball to the back-post area and would expect me to be there. When the ball came I knew it was a very good scoring opportunity and I had to make good contact. I had scored a number of goals with my head but I was never known as a great header of the ball. Now if the ball had come over and I had had to volley it, then I would have been so much more confident about scoring. That wasn't an option so I headed it confidently with power back across the keeper. It was a goal that gave me enormous satisfaction but I would have been incredibly disappointed if I'd missed it.

After I scored my momentum took me off the field into the discus circle where I fell. There was so much adrenaline flowing that I wouldn't have felt anything even if the circle had not been rubber!

In the dressing room at half-time it was no different to normal – the players were silent and listened to Clough. When he talked there had to be silence even when you were winning a European Cup final. You learnt as you went along that he was the Boss, that when he spoke nobody else spoke. He wasn't particularly pleased with the performance and he was looking for better in the second half.

I do remember that we were never in too much trouble. Indeed, at the start of the second half I beat the full-back and delivered a ball into the box, John came on to it and struck the upright. Had that gone in, it would have put us into a commanding position. But even at 1-0 we were fairly comfortable and although we had won there was a strange, subdued atmosphere after the game. You would never have thought that little Nottingham Forest had just won the European Cup.

I think there was a tinge of disappointment deep down for the Boss and Peter, because they were great believers in showcasing what they had achieved. They liked the game to be played along the carpet and they thought this was an opportunity for us to put on a memorable show. We were unable to do that and I think that's where the disappointment came from, even though they had just won a major trophy. There was no great euphoria which you would have expected. They wanted a classy performance. Even the post-match celebrations were subdued as we had a small meal with our wives afterwards minus the management team, who were not big on celebrations – they were already thinking about preparations for the next season. What a crazy game football is. I remember that seven days before the final, Larry Lloyd, John Robertson and I had scored as we beat Mansfield Town 3-1 to win the County Cup in front of 9,000 spectators in the City Ground. What a difference!

* * *

In my second season at Forest I felt so much more a part of things because I had won a trophy and played a few more games for England. But then I had to go over to Detroit to play a number of games. Whilst I was in the US I made the decision that, although this was only the second season of a three-year deal, I didn't want to go again. It was a nice little money earner the first year but the second year didn't turn out that way and unfortunately on my very last game over there I damaged my groin. That meant that I wasn't able to come back and immediately play for Nottingham Forest, much to the annoyance of the Boss. I was absent for about three weeks.

When I did start playing again I felt very much part of the furniture. Tony Woodcock had moved to Cologne so I was given the central striker's role. That was where I preferred to play and I always felt that it was where the Boss preferred me to play. I was also aware that Peter Taylor had strong team selection views. On one occasion Peter spoke about how he liked the contrast between John Robertson on the left, with his guile, trickery and ability to cross, and on the other side my searing pace and scoring ability. We could attack from both sides in different ways.

A very important game that season was the League Cup Final at Wembley against Wolverhampton Wanderers. We were red-hot favourites to win as we didn't lose too many finals under Clough.

Just prior to the final we had lost in the European Cup quarter-final first leg at the City Ground against Dynamo Berlin 1-0. This meant there was extra pressure on us to win at Wembley. On the morning of the game, the team was announced and the front four were Robertson, Birtles, Francis and O'Neill.

Wolves had an ageing back four. One of those players was Emlyn Hughes, who was in the twilight of his career. Surprisingly I started on the right wing with

Martin O'Neill playing as a central striker, perhaps due to Peter Taylor's influence. We lost the game 1-0 which was a surprise result, but a bigger surprise was the way the Boss switched all the attention and the blame on to me. My performance wasn't good enough, I accept that, but the big disappointment of losing at Wembley was made much worse when I woke up on the Sunday morning to read national newspaper headlines stating that the defeat was more or less my fault. I was not best pleased.

The squad set off on the Monday morning for the quarter-final second leg in Berlin. The media were talking about a 'crisis' based on our last two results and according to them we were just about to be knocked out of the European Cup as the holders.

We did our preparation as usual, which was mainly about how we would approach the game, then after that we went to look at the pitch. It was a bitterly cold night and as I was walking around the pitch Clough came up to me and said, 'Eh, young man, where do you want to play tonight?' I said, 'Boss, you know where I want to play – up the middle.' He replied, 'Right, you start there and make sure you finish the game there!' This confirmed to me that Clough recognised that this was an incredibly important game for everyone at the club, including him. This was his way of exerting his power – no one was going to influence him that night regarding team selection, not even Peter Taylor. After being 'blamed' for the League Cup defeat I had had no contact from Clough until 90 minutes before kick-off. He just had that way of keeping it short, sharp and to the point and giving me the opportunity to play where I wanted to play.

He got the response he wanted from me. By half-time the game was won, we were leading 3-0 and ended up winning 3-1 on aggregate. I got the first two goals and John Robertson scored a penalty. It was undoubtedly one of my finest days at Nottingham Forest. Whether Clough really blamed me I'll never know but what it did do was deflect any blame away from him, Peter Taylor and the rest of the players and pinned it firmly on me – another example of that ability he had to manage the media.

He was never one for coaching jargon – he used basic motivation techniques. He never overloaded players with information and sometimes I wonder how players can express themselves these days with so much 'shit' in their heads.

With the Boss it was straight to the point. It would be impossible to try and copy Clough because he was unique; he just had it. He never coached us but he never missed a thing on the field. At half-time or at the end of the match he would 'have' you if you had failed to perform to his standards.

For the semi-final we went up against Ajax who were a formidable side that included the defender Ruud Krol who never got the praise he deserved. For me he was up there with Franz Beckenbauer. We had won in Nottingham where I scored so we had to go to Amsterdam to defend a

2-0 lead to get to the final. We always used to go for a little walk after dinner and outside the hotel there were half a dozen Dutch fans who were taunting us. Clough got a lighter, probably from John Robertson, ran over to them, grabbed their flag and set fire to it. Amazing.

Our hotel was about a mile from the red light area and the two guys at the front went to turn around as they thought we had walked far enough. But the Boss and Peter told us to keep on walking. We were now in the red light area of Amsterdam the night before the semi-final of the European Cup. There were Ajax fans and Forest fans who could not believe it. Peter Taylor took us into a bar and ordered a beer for everyone – this was the night before a match, the supporters could not get their breath.

It was all part of the management trying to relax us.

The next day, for only the second time in my experience, I heard Clough talk about an opposing player. The first time it was Liam Brady and this time it was Ruud Krol. Clough always talked up his own players and there were never any negatives. In the first leg Krol had been outstanding, with the range of his passing just brilliant. What was ironic was that we were told by the local press that what Ajax were most concerned about was my pace and that we would play deep and then hit them on the counter-attack. Clough said he did not want Ruud Krol spraying passes around the pitch so he pointed at me and said, 'You, mark him.'

I'm thinking, I'm the big threat to Ajax and he's telling me to mark Krol. This is an example of the Boss saying it his way. In modern jargon it would be, 'Whenever Krol gets possession whoever is closest go and engage him, close him down and press.' But Clough said, 'Go and mark him.' It's something that's stuck with me for a long time. They played ever so well, Ajax, and they did beat us but Peter Shilton made one or two superb saves which enabled us to still go through to our second European Cup final in two years.

I was playing the best football of my career without a shadow of a doubt. The penultimate game of the league season was at home to Crystal Palace. Clough and Taylor were not at the game, they were away in Germany watching our European Cup Final opponents, Hamburg. I was on fire and playing in my favourite position of central striker. I had already scored two goals and was chasing a hat-trick and we were leading 4-0 with 20 minutes to go.

I was sprinting towards their goal when I suddenly pulled up and stumbled, clutching my ankle. I felt the most excruciating pain in my calf. It was like I had been shot by someone in the crowd. There was no contact with any player but I was carried off, taken to hospital and operated on the following day for a snapped Achilles tendon. That was the end of my season. The European Cup Final was only a couple of weeks away. The injury also meant that I missed playing for England in the 1980 European Championship. How ironic it was that in my first season at Forest, I had made the European final almost by default and in my second season I was going to miss out despite deserving to be there having fully played my part in our success. I was out of action for eight months, not playing again until a home match a week before Christmas 1980 against Sunderland in which I scored in our 3-1 victory.

Two weeks went by without any contact from Clough or Taylor – they didn't ring, send messages or come to the hospital. I came out of hospital after a few days and I had heard nothing from the football club. Soon after I had a telephone call from Clough's secretary, Carol, to say that I was not wanted at the final as it would be too much of a distraction for the rest of the players with me being on crutches. The Boss had obviously told her what to say. So my presence was not required which was totally against his idea of us being a group and all being in it together. I was incredibly upset.

I went on holiday and watched the game on television, which became one of the most surreal events of my life. I managed to get a little television in the basement of our small hotel in Cannes in the South of France and from there I watched the game. Even though the Boss didn't want me to go to the game I was delighted that Forest won the cup.

He made me feel like I was an outsider to the extent that I wasn't even invited to go on the open-top bus parade around Nottingham.

Clough was not alone in this attitude to injured players; Bill Shankly never used to speak to his Liverpool players when they were injured. Clough had the same mentality but it did not square with his ethos of all being one.

Four or five weeks had gone by so I rang the football club as I thought it made sense to see if Clough was available, because on that particular day Helen and I were going to make the long trip from our home in Newark down to the West Country to see my parents. I spoke to Carol and asked, 'Is the Boss there? I'm on my way to Plymouth to see my parents so can I come and see him?'

She obviously checked with him and called back to say I could call in on the way down. Helen drove and throughout the journey I was rehearsing in my mind what I wanted to say. I knew from his character that it was going to be quite a daunting experience going head to head with Brian Clough. Naturally I was delighted for the team and the management but I just felt poorly treated. I was going through in my mind what I was going to say and I was determined to tell him *exactly* how I felt.

I walked in and Clough immediately greeted me very warmly and the conversation went as follows:

BC: 'How are you, Trev?'

TF: 'Alright,' in a really low-key manner.

BC: 'I hear you are on your way to see your family in Plymouth.'

TF: 'Yeah.'

BC: 'I've got a friend who has got a beautiful hotel out on Dartmoor, you know?'

TF: 'Of course I know Dartmoor.'

BC: 'Do you ever take your mum and dad out for lunch?'

TF: 'Of course I do.'

BC: 'How about your brother and sister, do you take them as well?'

TF: 'Yes.'

BC: 'I want you to take the family out there. When you arrive have a nice glass of champagne and then order their best bottle of wine. Enjoy the lunch and send me the bill – it's all on me, young man!'

I looked at him and in a different tone of voice I said, 'Thank you very much, Boss,' shook his hand and walked out!

When I got back to the car Helen said, 'Did you tell him what you wanted to say?' and I said, 'Oh yes, I told him alright!'

I recovered from the Achilles problem and started to play well again but we were knocked out of Europe and Clough began to sell off many of the European Cup-winning players. To this day I have never quite understood why he wanted to sell me, Peter Shilton, John Robertson and Kenny Burns.

The European Super Cup does not get the recognition in this country that it does elsewhere in Europe. We won the 1979 Super Cup, beating Barcelona, the Cup Winners' Cup champions, 1-0. In the 1980 final we were playing Valencia and had the second leg approaching in December.

Once again my timing wasn't great as I had only just played my first comeback game after rupturing my Achilles tendon. After being out for eight months, it was a practice match against some of the apprentices down at the training ground. Playing against Valencia was not on my mind.

On the Monday we flew to Valencia and surprisingly to me I was in the squad. There were no expectations on my behalf. The Boss had told me to pack my boots and let's see what happens. This was a time when I was just getting myself back into the group.

Tuesday morning came and I did a little bit of training with the rest of the squad. Shortly after we had finished the Boss asked me if I fancied playing tennis that afternoon. To my mind this meant that I wasn't going to be involved in the second leg, because I was playing a game of tennis with Brian Clough.

Playing in the afternoon heat we had three sets. It was only supposed to be one set, but I won it so typically Clough wanted to play another set which he won. So at one set all we had to have a deciding set which I won!

We didn't train on the Wednesday when the Boss said to me late afternoon, 'How are you feeling?' I replied, 'A little tired after the game yesterday but it was a good competitive game, wasn't it?' Clough said, 'Yes, you played well and I want you to start tonight.'

He never ceased to surprise me. I was surprised that my boots were in the kit let alone me starting against Valencia but that was the Boss. Unpredictable in the extreme.

We lost the game that night 1-0 and Valencia won the trophy on the away goals rule.

It was mid-February 1981 when we travelled to Tokyo to play in the final of the World Club Championship against Nacional, the South American champions from Uruguay.

The match was staged midweek, between two league games, and to combat the time difference Clough had the idea that we all stay on English time. Considering this was the World Club Championship our preparation for the game was far from ideal, because, due to our body clocks being out of sync, I found myself walking around the streets of Tokyo with my team-mates in the early hours of the morning.

The playing surface was as bad as I've seen throughout my career. Many areas were just hard ground with little or no grass. Brian Clough, when addressing the world media, said that we could put men on the Moon but they couldn't grow grass in Japan. As you can imagine it was quite an experience and disappointing to lose to a single goal, particularly as we should have won the game.

The Uruguayans were in their close season and had not played a competitive match for four months, yet they took the lead after only ten minutes.

Happy to be ahead, like many South American teams they decided to sit back and absorb a huge amount of Forest pressure.

We fielded a strong side and played well in the second half but we failed to take advantage of a couple of opportunities that I created. Ian Wallace hit the side netting after I had put him in a shooting position and then I provided a cross that John Robertson headed wide.

The Tokyo crowd were nothing more than polite observers, and Nacional would have been more potent had they been in the middle of their season. On the whole, though, it was disappointing that Forest failed to become the first British club to win the title of world club champions.

It was in the summer of 1981 when a speculative double deal was mentioned which potentially gave me the opportunity to join Ron Atkinson at Old Trafford.

It was a complicated deal, which had been discussed between Ron and Brian Clough. The suggestion was that the Manchester United pair of goalkeeper Gary Bailey and ex-Forest striker Garry Birtles would be sold to Nottingham Forest in exchange for Peter Shilton and me plus a cash adjustment. I believe the cash adjustment was close to £1 million to be paid by United to Forest.

There is no doubt in my mind that both managers wanted the deal to happen but, close as it was to completion, the deal fell apart because there was no agreement on the 'cash' side of the transaction.

Shortly after, Ron tried to do a single deal with Forest to sign me. But he could not get it over the line with the Old Trafford board.

So there I was, close to becoming a Manchester United player on two separate occasions.

You have heard the expression that 'football is a funny old game'. Well, that was never more clear than two weeks later when I was signed by the club on the other side of Manchester.

Although everyone was aware of my potential move to United, there was never any animosity shown to me by either the local press or the City fans.

I was never looking to leave Forest – I was more than happy to stay there – but, when a manager makes it clear that he wants to sell you, my recommendation to any player is that it is best to go.

Peter Shilton was an exceptional goalkeeper and generated as many points from games through his saves as I did with my goals. He was a tremendous asset to the Forest team and he worked hard to achieve his success. I never knew a player that trained as hard as Peter.

It is regarding training that I mention Peter, as it brought out another side of Brian Clough's mentality.

It was the Friday before my Manchester City debut and I was still training at Forest.

The normal training session had ended but I decided to do some shooting practice. Without my asking, 'Shilts' volunteered to stand between the posts and we got on with things.

My shooting practice did not last long once Clough had seen what was happening.

He asked me what I was doing to which I replied I was getting in some shooting practice.

Clough replied: 'Not with my goalkeeper you're not. Go and get your own!'

I had the greatest respect for Peter Shilton and he was undoubtedly the best keeper I ever played with, making countless saves that won us numerous points.

It made me realise the importance of a top goalkeeper and I was fortunate in my career to play with some very good ones.

Joe Corrigan of Manchester City was an excellent goalkeeper and had an imposing stature. Unfortunately for Joe he was playing at the same time as Peter Shilton and Ray Clemence and therefore never got the number of caps his talent deserved – only nine in a six-year spell.

Even in Italy I had a very good goalkeeper – Ivano Bordon of Sampdoria, who was the understudy of the great Dino Zoff in the Italian national team.

And I can't forget the year I had at Glasgow Rangers with a number of top-quality English players including Chris Woods in goal.

When I went into football management I was conscious of the need for my team to have a good keeper. This had been something that I experienced under Brian Clough and, whilst I could never copy Clough's management techniques, I did commit some of his ideas to memory and the need for a strong first line of defence was one of them.

Therefore, in my first managerial role at Queens Park Rangers, I was more than happy to have David Seaman as my number one. His performances were being recognised throughout football and I was aware that, at almost every game, Arsenal had representatives watching him. I received two very good offers for his services from George Graham, the manager of Arsenal.

Of course it was my duty to relay these offers to my chairman along with my recommendation that they should be refused. The chairman supported me but shortly after turning down these offers I was sacked by the club. Interestingly, after my departure, David became an Arsenal player. George was a man who did not take no for an answer.

When I was appointed manager at Hillsborough one of my first signings was Chris Woods from Rangers, which surprised people at Sheffield Wednesday because we already had two good goalkeepers in Chris Turner and Kevin Pressman. But knowing that Woods had become available I could not resist the opportunity to bring England's number one to Hillsborough.

Chapter Five

Manchester City FC

In all senior competitions:
29 appearances; 14 goals

MY move from Nottingham Forest took place right at the end of season 1979/80 and I couldn't understand why I was being sold. The fans couldn't understand it and even one of the directors came up to me and said, 'Listen, if you don't want to go, you stay here.'

Whilst I did not doubt his sincerity I realised that only one voice mattered at the City Ground.

When any manager decides it is time for you to go then it's time to go.

During late summer John Bond came to see me at Forest and offered me a three-year contract worth £100,000 a year plus bonuses. I was on my way to Maine Road, signing on 3 September 1981.

That season, I have to say, was a thoroughly enjoyable time. John was a very good coach and I enjoyed working with him, particularly as it was the first time in my career, at the age of 27, that I was given professional forward coaching.

He was very good on the training field and, whilst a lot of my play was natural, I learnt more in that one year at Maine Road than I had in the whole of my footballing career up until then.

I developed a great relationship with the Manchester City fans during my time there, becoming a big favourite.

My first game was away at Stoke where we had a travelling contingent of 7,000. We performed well and I managed to score two goals in our victory. It was the perfect start to my time there and the fans never forgot that day.

It was all going well and after winning the last game of 1981 against Wolverhampton Wanderers we went to the top of Division One.

It is my belief that if the club had strengthened with two or three players in the following January then we could have challenged for the Championship. I remember Martin O'Neill telling me not long after he signed for City that according to John Bond he was intended to be the first of several major transfers that season and that players of the calibre of Joe Jordan and Justin Fashanu were targeted, but nothing materialised.

In fact, the opposite happened and the club got itself into financial difficulties, a couple of players were sold and we slipped out of contention.

As well as the good days there will always be the bad days, and one such day was the time I was sent off for the only time in my career.

It is a blemish on my disciplinary record that I regret and remember to this day.

It was a home game against Everton and I made a challenge on Neville Southall, which was late, and both of us ended up on the ground.

I was immediately surrounded by Everton players which created an intimidating situation, with at least three of them jostling me and letting me know in no uncertain terms what they felt about my challenge on their keeper. As I got myself to my feet, and as a reaction to the position I was in, I put my head into the face of Billy Wright.

There was no real force in the gesture, we just touched heads, but he took full advantage of the situation and fell to the ground. On the face of it, the referee had no option but to send me off – no red cards in those days.

I've looked at the incident on many occasions since and I must admit that the movement of my head suggests that it was a head butt, but 40 years on I can categorically state that there was no force or intention to hurt anyone.

But it doesn't matter now. The referee made the call and I was off and banned for three games. The referee was Derek Civil from Great Barr in Birmingham, which is an Aston Villa part of the city. I know that Derek acted as referee at Villa Park for a number of friendlies and I just wonder if I was sent off by a Villa supporter?

At the end of the season, I went off to play for England in the 1982 World Cup. When I returned, I received a call from Sampdoria to see if I was interested in joining them.

My move, which I guess was due to the financial crisis being experienced by the club, was a huge surprise to me. I was happy at Manchester City and was looking forward to going back for a second season.

Chapter Six

Italy

Serie A Sampdoria: 68 senior appearances; 17 goals
Serie A Atalanta: 21 senior appearances; 1 goal

SAMPDORIA had been watching me during the 1982 World Cup. They had just got promoted from the Italian second division and the regulations allowed them to bring in two foreign players. Having watched me a couple of times they secured my services at the same time as Liam Brady joined from Juventus.

This reaffirmed my belief in fate or good fortune. Due to the absence of Kevin Keegan with a back injury, I had played more games in the World Cup than I would have played had Kevin been fit. I played in five games for England, three in Bilbao and two in Madrid, starting in every one.

I looked up to Kevin Keegan. For me he was one of the best attacking players I had ever seen. I used to admire his application, his professionalism, his attitude, his effort and often thought his technical ability was never really appreciated. He was a great all-round player and I am convinced that the only action I would have seen, had he been fit, would have been from the bench or possibly playing in a wide area. Eventually he got himself fit for the last game of the tournament, when he came on as a substitute against Spain.

Thinking back, life is all about ifs and buts and taking your opportunities when they present themselves. I probably wouldn't have played in Italy if Kevin had been fully fit. That's what I believe.

I went to Italy because I received an offer that was too good to refuse. Their approach was a surprise because it had never been part of my thought process to go to Italy. I knew very quickly after signing how happy I was, and that it was the right decision. The environment we lived in was fantastic, the football was the best in Europe and in terms of profile, I was playing against some of the best players in the world – and I was being paid handsomely.

When I joined, Sampdoria had just returned to Serie A. In signing me, the president, Paolo Mantovani, was making a real statement of intent and we made a spectacular start to the 1982/83 Serie A campaign. We won our first three games which included a home win against Juventus, a side that boasted seven Italian 1982 World Cup squad members (Dino Zoff, Claudio Gentile, Antonio Cabrini, Marco Tardelli, Paolo Rossi and Gaetano Scirea plus Michel Platini and Zbigniew Boniek), Roma, who fielded Bruno Conti and the Brazilian midfielder Falcao, and an Inter Milan side that included Giuseppe Bergomi, Fulvio Collovati and Alessandro Altobelli.

The victories were unexpected and I made a positive impression. After just 11 minutes against Inter, with the game at 0-0, I set off from my own half, moving at pace and beating any defender that tried to stop me. Having reached the edge of the penalty area, I played a one-two with Roberto Mancini and fired my shot into the bottom corner. It was an incredible start, particularly as we went on to win the game 2-1 thanks to a Mancini volley.

An unfortunate incident occurred between myself and Roberto Mancini.

Prior to going on to the pitch for a pre-season friendly game I was told by the mister that I would be taking the penalties. Sure enough a penalty was awarded.

I took a hold of the ball and walked towards the penalty spot when Mancini came over and wrestled the ball away from me, saying that he was going to take the penalty.

Needless to say I was not best pleased. I reacted and a tussle ensued which ultimately was quite embarrassing for myself, the club and the mister.

Anyway, after what seemed some time, Mancini took the penalty kick and it was saved.

The atmosphere, as you can imagine, was toxic between the two of us and after the game, when we went into the dressing-room, I immediately approached Mancini to try and sort things out. There was a lot of pushing and shoving and then a few punches were thrown.

Other players saw what was happening and got involved to ultimately restore calm.

The incident was put to the back of our minds by both of us and there were no further recriminations but it clearly indicated to everyone involved that I do not accept things just for a quiet life.

Having said that, some defenders did manage to stop me and one I particularly remember was the Roma defender Pietro Vierchowod, who was part of the Italian 1982 World Cup squad. He was well known for his rugged approach and became a team-mate at Sampdoria the following year. One of his challenges sidelined me for several weeks and, as a result, Sampdoria's impressive form tailed off. The injury hampered me for the rest of the season and we eventually finished in seventh place.

Italy was a wonderful place for my family. Helen settled down very quickly and my son Matthew went to school there, making his first language Italian. Towards the end of my time in Italy in 1987, Helen fell pregnant with James.

My two years playing alongside Liam Brady were great both on and off the pitch. Liam, who was fluent in Italian having spent time at Juventus, really helped me settle in. When he was about to move to Inter after two years at the club, Mantovani, the president, got me to commit to another two years. Obviously he did not want to lose me but he also knew my re-signing would help him in his search for another foreign player to replace Liam.

Mantovani was interested in signing one of my close pals, Bryan Robson. Naturally I gave a great endorsement of Bryan. On an occasion when Bryan was injured, he and his wife came over to Genoa to spend a few days with Helen and me. They were there to spend time with their friends not with a view to joining an Italian club, as it was rumoured.

Ron Atkinson was manager at Manchester United and he was a huge fan of Bryan. In fact if you asked Ron who was his favourite player it would be Bryan Robson. I can understand why – Bryan was an outstanding midfield player. At the time he was in the thoughts of Mantovani he had not long been with United since joining them from West Bromwich Albion, so was always going to be a bit of a long shot. Anyway, Ron priced him out of the market!

Going into the last week of the Italian transfer window Mantovani asked me if I could think of anyone else. Without hesitation I told him, 'Get yourself up to the Olympic Stadium in Rome and look at Graeme Souness, who is captaining Liverpool in the European Cup Final against Roma.' He obviously liked what he saw and signed him for Sampdoria.

I did not know Graeme at that time so it was a recommendation based entirely on his footballing ability. He was highly thought of as a player. During our time together in Italy we became great friends and since then, throughout my time in football, we have enjoyed a close relationship.

We lived in Nervi on the Ligurian coast near Portofino, in a big villa that had been converted into five apartments. Graeme and I had ground floor flats opposite each other in the complex. My back garden overlooked the Mediterranean and literally ran down to it. It was just idyllic. Graeme and I did everything together – we travelled together, sat alongside each other on the team coach and we roomed together both at home and away matches. This went on for two years. We were also close socially and used to eat out two or three times a week with our wives. It would be fair to say that we are very, very good friends.

At the start of our first season together we upset the mister (which is coach or manager in England). For pre-season we would go away for three weeks to a training camp and to play friendly games against local opposition.

Everything was very regimented and we always had to be back in our rooms by 10 o'clock at night. The daily procedure was that we would get a wake-up call at 6 o'clock in the morning. An hour later we would all have breakfast together then go straight out for our morning training session. Afterwards we came back to shower and change.

Everything was prescribed: what we ate for breakfast, lunch and dinner and the times we ate. It was also insisted upon that whenever we ate, we would all sit down together.

Lunch was always finished by 2 o'clock when we had to return to our rooms to rest.

The afternoon training session started at 5 o'clock and lasted for an hour and a half.

It was dinner at 7 o'clock. It was all very disciplined to the extent that our food and drinks were overseen by the medical team.

Something which struck both Graeme and I was the respect everyone had for one another. For instance, when eating, nobody was allowed to leave the table until the captain had looked down the table to ensure everybody had finished. He then sought permission from the mister for us to leave the table. The mister would then make the decision as to whether we could leave or not.

This was all new to us but the Italian players accepted it as part of their lives and therefore we did the same.

We were allowed to go for a short walk after dinner and many players took the opportunity to have an espresso. But you were still expected to be back in your room by between 9.30 and 9.45. When we were all back in our rooms the doctor would come to see if anyone wanted anything before we went to bed.

During the third week of the training camp, Graeme fancied going down to the little village near our hotel. It wasn't late – about 9pm. We had a couple of beers and a pizza between us and it was just after 10 o'clock when we arrived back at the hotel. The mister was standing at the door. Although Graeme couldn't speak Italian, I am sure he got the sense that the mister wasn't particularly thrilled that we'd been out. Anyway, the mister called a meeting for the following morning, bringing all the players together to inform them that Graeme and I had broken the curfew rules. He made it clear that if this was to happen again then he would have to inform the president as this was the type of behaviour the club could not accept.

Graeme asked me what the mister was saying. I said it was nothing but Graeme knew better than that and repeated his question to me. I still did not tell Graeme, hoping not to inflame the situation. I failed because Graeme then said, 'Tell him I've just spoken to my kids, of which I have three back in Nervi, and they are all playing football out in the garden at 10 o'clock! Here I am, 32 years of age, I've won three European Cups so I don't need him telling me what to do!' I said, 'No, just leave it.'

When the mister said that if it happened again he would tell the president, Graeme said to me, 'Tell him it will fucking happen again!' The point Graeme wanted to make was that he'd been all over the world, he'd got kids, so he shouldn't be treated like a baby – he was a senior professional.

About three weeks later we were playing Palermo in Sicily in the Coppa Italia and the team had its own private plane to take us down to the afternoon game. We won the game and afterwards at the airport Graeme and I bought ourselves four small cans of beer. We sat at the front of the plane, trying to keep a low profile as we quietly opened a can each. To be honest I did not think it was such a serious offence, but it wasn't received very well and the captain came down, as the mister had seen us and wasn't happy. When we got off the plane we were informed that the mister was going to speak to the president and subsequently we had to go to see Mantovani.

I think the mister's recommendation was to get rid of us. The president did not go that far but he did fine us two weeks' salary and warned us that it could not happen again. I couldn't help but think about my time in England and some of the things the English footballers got up to hardly made this a criminal offence. But Graeme had been proved right – it did happen again!

The following campaign, season 1983/84, I returned with a bang, producing one of the performances of the season away at Inter, a side that must have been sick of the sight of me. With Inter leading 1-0 I seemed to take matters into my own hands and scored two second-half goals to earn us another famous victory. My performance led Inter's legendary goalkeeper Walter Zenga to say, 'Francis is the best forward I've ever seen.'

Walter and I were fellow pundits as part of beIN Sports' coverage of the World Cup 2018 in Russia.

Towards the end of the second season with Graeme, he had a call from Glasgow sounding him out about becoming the Rangers manager, and ultimately that's what he did, never completing his final year in Italy.

I remember Graeme sending one of his colleagues/ scouts from Liverpool to go and have a look at the Rangers team for him. The word came back that he needed nine players!

Graeme wasn't a great student of the game. He could never understand why I was so keen on watching football on the TV and in those days there was a lot of football on Italian television, far more than in England. But Graeme was not like me as I was an avid watcher.

I think he'd be the first to admit that with some of his early signings for Rangers I played a helping hand. He had been given more or less carte blanche to bring in players and with plenty of money to spend he would often ask my opinion on players that he was considering.

On one occasion we had flown down to Naples to play Maradona's Napoli. As usual it was a Sunday game but we got there on the Friday so in the afternoon we would be in our room with me giving Graeme my opinion on certain players. 'What about goalkeepers?' he asked. I said, 'Well, try for Peter Shilton.' When he couldn't get Shilton, my response was, 'What about Chris Woods?'

As we know, Chris Woods became the Rangers keeper. I then talked to Graeme about Terry Butcher, the central defender who also joined the club. I guess my role was simply to keep suggesting names of players that could suit his plans.

Sampdoria were doing well, having qualified for Europe after winning the Italian Cup. We had beaten AC

Milan and therefore were in the European Cup Winners' Cup of 1985. As well as doing well in that competition we were always going to play a part in which team would win Serie A.

Towards the end of the season we were at home to Juventus in Genoa and in with a chance of qualifying for the UEFA Cup. We were drawing the match. The game was vitally important to both teams as there were only three games left in the season and Juventus had a great chance to win the league. It was a game that neither team could afford to lose. As is customary with Italian football neither team was prepared to take too many risks. So the game was unexciting to say the least. At half-time, going up the steps to the dressing rooms, I was aware that two experienced players from both sides were in deep conversation what they said I do not know but it suited both teams to play the game to a draw.

That would be difficult to achieve in English football because of the way we play the game, but it was not so difficult in Italy as no one had a shot on goal! Juventus won the 1985/86 Serie A with Roma second and Napoli third.

Is that cheating? I've told this story only once or twice before, in private with very, very close friends. They were appalled by it. This is a reaction I understand, but perhaps it's because I played football in Italy for five years that, whilst I know it's not 100 per cent correct, the Italians do not see it as cheating. They see it as opportunistic.

Italy could not have been better; playing there was an incredible experience. I enjoyed my time in Italy very much because you have to remember that in 1982 Italy won the World Cup.

Italy has always been a football-mad nation but after that triumph we saw an unprecedented influx of foreign players. When I joined Sampdoria, other Italian clubs were also bringing in foreign players – the likes of Boniek and Platini – that calibre of player, and later Zico, Maradona, Socrates and Rummenigge – the list was endless. There were some wonderful players – it was like a who's who of football.

Every team in Serie A had a strict dress code and Sampdoria were no different. Every player received a full set of formal clothes emblazoned with the club badge: trousers, shirt, tie and blazer plus a large overcoat for use in the winter.

Graeme Souness came to Sampdoria in my third year in Italy. A natural prankster, Graeme never let his inability to understand Italian get in the way of his natural sense of humour.

Teams are made up of lots of different personalities and Graeme found himself in the same side as another keen prankster – Gianluca Vialli.

They often played tricks on their fellow team-mates but also on each other. As is often the case, once in a while a prank went too far and on this occasion Graeme overstepped the mark.

We were in Milan and had just enjoyed a pre-match meal before the fixture against AC Milan. As was customary, a number of us decided to take a stroll after our meal. We ended up by a lake on which there were a number of swans. Vialli took off his club tie, made it into a lasso and then pretended to try and lasso one of the swans.

It was a simple light-hearted moment that we were all enjoying but we were all unaware of Graeme coming behind Gianluca.

Souness did no more than push Vialli into the lake.

The reaction from the players was mixed: some laughed but others were quite shocked. I guess the most important reaction was from Gianluca himself. What did he do? He smiled and went to the match soaking wet!

During my time with Sampdoria, Fabio Capello said this about me: 'He was the best Englishman to have played in Italy.' I was very pleased to hear this. To receive a compliment from a man of his great stature both in England and Italy filled me with pride.

* * *

After four years at Sampdoria it was clear that I was not going to be retained for the following season. But I enjoyed myself so much in Italy that I was in no hurry to come back to England. I was lucky enough to have my Italian adventure extended when I went to Atalanta in Bergamo. It was a totally different experience to Sampdoria. Why? Because here I was in a team that clearly set out its stall from the very first match. Its objective was to stay in the league. This meant I played as the lone striker and therefore, from a footballing point of view, it was not a particularly enjoyable time. I enjoyed Bergamo and continued to enjoy the Italian lifestyle of which I was very much a part, but the football was different. It was a struggle and I only scored one goal.

Ironically my first game for Atalanta was away against Sampdoria and I was given the lone striker's role. In the opening few minutes a number of our players were already wasting time. Clearly our intention was to get a goalless draw. After 20 minutes out came the first yellow card and, you've guessed it, it was for time-wasting. That really set the pattern for the rest of the season.

It was not a memorable season as we were relegated to Serie B but we did get to the two-leg final of the Coppa Italia against Napoli. At the time I was suffering with a dislocated shoulder that kept reoccurring and although I could have played in the final they allowed me to go into hospital for a corrective operation. This showed the low regard held for the Coppa Italia compared with the league competition.

I have to laugh about the circumstances surrounding my only goal. They had a ruling in Italy, which no longer applies, that if a game is called off on a Sunday the away team stays in town and the game is played the following day. The game was Atalanta against Fiorentina and it was called off because of a snow storm which made the pitch unplayable. So I poke fun at myself because the only goal

I scored for the club was on a Monday afternoon! Good quiz question?

After my fourth year in Italy there was speculation about my future and I received a phone call from the then chairman of Aston Villa, Doug Ellis. He told me he was very interested in me joining Aston Villa and he immediately made me a financial offer.

As with all these types of offers, you need to consider two things. Firstly, is the offer genuine, which means is it made without any ulterior motive, such as publicity/press coverage? Secondly, is the offer good enough from a financial point of view? If it is not, then you have to make a judgement as to whether the offer could be increased if you showed interest.

In analysing Doug's offer I came to the conclusion very quickly that it was a good offer but not a great one. I then considered the fact that even if it had been a great offer, could I allow myself to go to Aston Villa?

Without further hesitation I knew for me it was an impossible move, regardless of any financial benefit. Trevor Francis wearing the claret and blue of Aston Villa? Never. I declined the offer politely.

Chapter Seven

Glasgow Rangers FC

All senior competitions: 11 appearances,
12 substitute appearances; 0 goals

MY time was up in Italy – I was 33 years of age and looking to continue my career back in England. I suppose it was no surprise that Glasgow Rangers, in the form of my friend Graeme Souness, were interested in signing me to be part of the revolution that was happening at Ibrox.

Graeme, who was the first player-manager in Rangers' history, could see me playing a part in what he was trying to create. I felt I was already part of his achievement as I had suggested several players to him whilst we were in Italy, which he had subsequently signed.

Now I was about to make the decision to go and join him in Glasgow.

Glasgow was a city I liked very much.

In Glasgow religion is a much bigger issue than in England and the split between Rangers and

Celtic was never more obvious than in the following two incidents.

Collar and tie was the dress code at Rangers for training, which was a long-held tradition. As I was leaving training one day, suited and booted as usual, there were, as is normally the case, a number of fans waiting for autographs. This was well before the selfie era of today.

This young lad asked me to sign his autograph book and gave me his pen. I was just about to sign my name when his father intervened.

His intervention was stern and aggressive and related to the pen his son had given me, which contained green ink!

The father was angry that a Rangers fan, his son, would ask a Rangers player to write his autograph in green – the colour of Celtic.

The impact of colour was also clearly evidenced on the snooker tables at Ibrox, where the traditional green baize had been replaced with Rangers blue. Amazing.

Sectarian mentality also existed elsewhere. Helen and I were looking for somewhere to live and had identified two beautiful developments in Bothwell, where we eventually settled down.

We were looking at a particular residence when the workers came over to us, obviously recognising me, and made it quite clear that the property we were looking at had been allocated to Mick McCarthy of Celtic. They stressed that we would be better off looking at the other development, as the one we were at was for Catholics and the other was for Protestants or non-Catholics.

It was a brand new experience for both Helen and I as we had never previously experienced any divisions in a community due to religion.

Graeme told me privately that one day he would 'shock football' by signing a Catholic player for Rangers. He kept his promise when he signed Mo Johnston in July 1989. I had left Ibrox the previous March so I never experienced first-hand the reaction from the Rangers fans to having a Catholic player in their team. It must have been something because I recall him needing security when he moved around the city.

It was such an eye-opener playing football in Glasgow because I was surprised by the size of Glasgow Rangers as a football club and the passion shown by the Glasgow Rangers supporters. I guess it shouldn't have been that much of a surprise as I had witnessed England v Scotland matches over the years. For me it was the nearest you could get to the passion shown by Italian fans.

Going there from Atalanta, I knew that Graeme's thinking was that, as Rangers were in the European Cup, my experience in both European club and international football would be invaluable to his team.

My time there was frustrating because I was used very sparingly by Graeme. It had nothing to do with my fitness, as throughout my spell there my fitness levels were high. My years in Italy coupled with my attitude of being a good professional in terms of diet and lifestyle had made me fitter than I had ever been in my career.

The Italian type of training and the fewer games played in a season all contributed to this and I came to Glasgow Rangers obviously looking to do well, create a good impression and enjoy the European Cup matches, but I was rarely played on a Saturday. I only made 18 league appearances of which eight were starts, whilst the remaining ten were me coming off the bench. I proved in training time and time again that I was very fit, still very sharp and that I had a huge appetite to play.

I felt that I should have been used more often and my frustration levels grew. I wanted to speak to Graeme but that was never going to be easy because of our friendship. I found it difficult but what surprised me was that Graeme found it even more difficult.

One time, the two of us were in a sauna at Ibrox chatting when Graeme announced that he would never sign a friend again. He didn't need to say any more; I knew exactly what he meant by that. I asked him to agree that if we went out of European competition he would allow me to move on – as a friend he agreed.

I was not the only England international who went to play for Graeme at Rangers: Chris Woods, Terry Butcher, Ray Wilkins, Mark Hateley and Trevor Steven immediately come to mind. In keeping with Graeme's belief that 'big clubs need big players' he also signed Graham Roberts, Richard Gough and Mark Walters.

I won a medal at Hampden Park when we won the League Cup against Aberdeen. I came on as substitute, no surprise there, and it went to penalties. I put myself forward to take one. It was against Jim Leighton, who made over 380 senior appearances in 17 years. I had a technique where I took two steps and then shot. I scored and got christened 'Trevor Two Step' by the media and fans.

Although I never scored in normal time for Rangers I do claim a significant assist. It was in the second leg of round one of the European Champions' Cup. We were 0-1 down to Dynamo Kiev after the first leg which was played in front of a crowd of 100,000 in the Republic Stadium. On 30 September 1987 at Ibrox we were all-square at 1-1 after Mark Falco's goal. Then midway through the second half I crossed the ball for Mark to head on to Ally McCoist, who headed home the winner. The game was also remembered for Graeme arranging for the touchlines to be moved in a yard or two to narrow the field. It was all done within the legally required measurements of course. This helped to restrict the pace of the Russians' wide players. Dynamo weren't best pleased by this gamesmanship on Graeme's part.

My Rangers team-mate Ray 'Butch' Wilkins had lived next door to me in Bowdon, Cheshire when I played for Manchester City and he was with United. Our careers coincided several times thereafter.

Ray had also been in Italy when I was there playing for AC Milan. We then spent 12 months together when we returned to the UK to join Glasgow Rangers. At that time we lived opposite each other.

When I was manager of Queens Park Rangers I signed him on the day I got the sack so we never got to work together at Loftus Road. He stayed there as a player until 1994 when he was appointed player-manager, replacing another Francis, Gerry.

How sad I felt when he died in 2018 at such an early age. We had a strong connection as I played more times with him for England than any other player. A great loss.

Throughout football, fans talk about which are the fiercest of local derbies: Aston Villa v Birmingham City, Liverpool v Everton, Manchester United v Manchester City, Arsenal v Tottenham Hotspur or Sheffield United v Sheffield Wednesday, and the list goes on and on.

Let me tell you that in my experience nothing compares to the Glasgow derby, whether it is played at Ibrox or Celtic Park.

The atmosphere that is generated is the absolute best and nothing rivals it.

Playing in that atmosphere is something special, as you are subject to some intimidating tackles, a frantic pace and flying challenges that could be dangerous.

These are games where technical forwards have to work extremely hard to triumph over strong, determined defenders.

On 17 October 1987 a fierce 2-2 draw was played out at Ibrox during which three players were sent off. It all kicked off as early as the 17th minute when McAvennie clipped Woods around the ear which provoked him to retaliate by hitting Frank in the face with his elbow. That was bad enough but then Butcher joined in by pushing Frank away before Graham Roberts steamed in and grabbed McAvennie by the throat and knocked him to the ground. McAvennie and Woods were sent off for the initial incident, whilst Butcher was sent off later in the game. Graham Roberts had to take over from Woods between the sticks.

If that wasn't enough all four men were later reported to the procurator fiscal and appeared in court on disorder charges relating to their conduct in the game.

McAvennie was found not guilty and in Roberts' case it was not proven; Butcher and Woods were both convicted of breach of the peace.

There is no doubt that this football match created legal precedents throughout the United Kingdom; there was a definite involvement from central government to put football in its place as far as its influence on the behaviour of the fans.

Driven by this political agenda, the players involved were subjected to far closer scrutiny than would normally be the case. Frank McAvennie thought things were far-fetched, as indeed they were, and wondered why the police were suddenly involved in a football game.

The incidents that occurred were the sort of thing that happened in football games up and down the country every week. As always when local rivalry is involved, the tension is heightened and the players are a bit hyped up.

The altercation between Woods and McAvennie could have been deemed unnecessarily aggressive but so much of the sectarian-scarred contests in those days were like that.

Many fans at the time felt that it all added to the football spectacle – nothing like a bit of aggro to get the crowd going!

Indeed Andy Walker, who opened the scoring for Celtic in the 33rd minute, described it as 'the best Old Firm game I ever played in'.

No quarter was asked from any of the players, and right from the moment when McAvennie bundled Woods into the net because he liked 'hitting keepers' until the 92nd minute – when emergency goalkeeper Roberts conducted a rendition of 'The Sash' by Rangers fans once Richard Gough had netted a last-gasp equaliser for a home side who had been 2-0 down – it was a raw battle between two sides demanding 100% commitment.

Terry Butcher was constantly in the thick of it. Booked for his part in the defining melee, he deflected the ball into his own net for the 35th-minute counter that led Peter Grant to celebrate by blessing himself in front of the Celtic support. Finally, Butcher was sent off, shortly after Ally McCoist had pulled a goal back in the 65th minute.

As was predicted at the time, people now ask how these incidents ended up in court – what was it all about?

Butcher thought it was about the sinister desire of the British government to put football and footballers in their place. The hooliganism that blighted the 1980s, most shamefully at Heysel in 1985, had caused the sport to be viewed in political circles as a stain on society.

Terry was quoted in *The Scotsman* as saying,'I have no doubt that there was government interference and pressure applied from the highest level to bring convictions against us. We were convenient scapegoats, we were the role models who had to be slapped down and told how to behave so that the supporters would get the message. It was pathetic, but made for a nightmare time as the legal wheels turned.'

The situation was made worse by the game's officialdom. Many believed that the referee, Jake Duncan, panicked and he suffered the consequences of his poor decision as it seems he never took charge of another high-profile game during his career. McAvennie recalls: 'I remember when he showed Chris the red, I thought "God, that's harsh" as I waited for a yellow. When he then sent me off as well, I just could not believe it.'

Soon after, the two club chairmen, David Holmes of Rangers and Jack McGinn of Celtic, held a lengthy meeting at which they discussed possible action. Glasgow's Procurator Fiscal, Sandy Jessop, went into action and, on 1 November, the quartet were summoned to Govan police station to face the charge of 'conduct likely to provoke a breach of the peace among spectators'.

Over the next couple of weeks, suspicions firmed up that the worldwide publicity the case was attracting merely strengthened the prosecutor's determination to press for convictions. The two clubs agreed a joint defence and appointed one of Scotland's best-known solicitors, Len Murray, to represent the players.

From the court records:

On 20 November, the charge against the players was refined to 'while participating in a football match, you did conduct yourself in a disorderly manner and commit a breach of the peace'. The trial began on 12 April 1988. The assistant chief constable of Strathclyde, John Dickson, spent a day on the witness stand giving the impression that the actions of McAvennie, Woods, Butcher and Roberts had come dangerously close to provoking public disorder on a grand scale: 'There was unbridled hatred on the faces of some of the fans when they were shouting obscenities and insults at each other.' Without enlisting reinforcements in response to the incident, Dickson insisted a pitch invasion would have ensued.

Passing sentence, Sheriff Archibald McKay said Woods' involvement had been much more serious than the others, stating that video 'clearly established that you jabbed McAvennie on the chin with your left forearm. It was an assault which constituted breach of the peace.' The sheriff also deemed Butcher guilty of a 'violent push ... which might reasonably have been expected to upset other Celtic players and their support'. In summing up, he damned all the co-defendants, who sat in the dock together. 'A large percentage of supporters are readily converted by breaches of the peace into two rival mobs. That they were not so transformed is no credit to you. You must have been aware of your wider responsibilities and you failed to discharge them.'

Chapter Eight

Queens Park Rangers FC

*As both player and player-manager:
40 senior appearances, two substitute
appearances, 15 goals*

PLAYING at Queens Park Rangers was similar to being back in Detroit. In other words playing on AstroTurf. The trouble was that it was not the best playing surface as some of the seams were splitting which meant that sand was leaking out from under the AstroTurf. This was because the contract was coming to an end and the pitch was being allowed to deteriorate.

I was a player from March 1988 and became player-manager in the December. At the beginning of the 1988/89 season I was given the responsibility of taking the penalties and ironically the first one was awarded against my old club, Sheffield Wednesday. I converted it successfully, adopting the same technique I'd used to score at Hampden Park in the Scottish League Cup Final against Aberdeen in the penalty shoot-out. At the time, I felt that goalkeepers were getting away with moving too early before the kick was taken. I decided to counteract this by adopting my two-step method, as the quickness of my movement would prevent them from moving early.

Unfortunately that was quickly undone by successive penalty misses.

After the second miss the press spoke to Jim Smith about my penalty-taking technique which they acknowledged was an unusual way of taking a spot kick. When questioned about it, Jim Smith's response was typical of the man. He said, 'Well, obviously his technique isn't fucking working!'

Managing a football club had never been high on my agenda but of course as my playing career was coming to an end due to my age I did start to consider my future options.

It was during my final season at Ibrox that it became common knowledge through the football grapevine that Jim Smith, who was managing Queens Park Rangers, wanted me to return south of the border. At the time I did think it was slightly ironic that the man who had sold me for £1 million in 1979 was now, almost ten years later, wanting to get me on a free transfer.

Jim was one of the few managers who achieved the distinction of managing more than a thousand games. He was acknowledged as being one of the most popular personalities in football.

He had this ability to have a go at you immediately after a game whether it was an individual he was singling out or the team performance.

He was never slow to throw cups and other things and use expletives in his blunt Yorkshire accent. But after about three-quarters of an hour when we were heading home on the coach it would all be forgotten. He would be in the middle of the coach surrounded by players, drinking beer, telling stories and jokes. A special manager and a special man.

He had many strengths but the one which I particularly admired was his honesty, which was never better demonstrated than by the way he handled my transfer from Birmingham City to Nottingham Forest.

Because of the limited game time I had had under Graeme I felt that moving to Loftus Road would give me the opportunity to prove that I still had a lot to offer as a professional footballer. I was determined to prove Graeme was wrong – not in a nasty way because I have a lot of feeling for Graeme – but I wanted to get out on to the pitch and show him and the footballing world that I still had the fitness and skill I had always possessed. Then, perhaps, he might look back and think that possibly he should have played me more often.

Of course, this attitude could only prove valuable to QPR. How did I do?

In answering that question, I could quote you the relevant statistics but the real measure of how well

I was playing can be evidenced by the fact that in my mid-thirties the London media, who were particularly influential in those days, were calling for my recall into the England team. I have to say that I was delighted with the publicity my football was getting at that time in my playing career.

But with everything going well, Jim made the announcement that he was leaving to take on the manager's role at Newcastle United. Naturally I was disappointed, because Jim and I had always got on well both in and outside of football. That was surprise number one. I did not have to wait long for surprise number two: I was offered the player-manager's job! Could I do it?

It was December 1988 and a critical time for any club, as decisions made around Christmas often have a major impact on the club's final league position. Could I make a difference in such a short space of time?

The answer to my dilemma was based on my experiences with Graeme in Scotland. Whatever I thought of his selection choices there was no doubt that he had a successful time in Glasgow. He was regarded as one of the very top managers in British football and I had no quarrel with that assessment, but I knew from my experiences under him that football management was not going to be easy. This was my chance to go and see what I could do as the manager of a top London club, because there was no doubt in my mind that watching Graeme had given me a bit of an appetite for football management.

So I agreed to take on the role, much to the disappointment of Peter Shreeves, who had been appointed caretaker manager after Jim's departure.

Eventually Don Howe joined me as assistant manager.

I was full of confidence upon my appointment to the hot seat but quickly realised I was now on a massive learning curve. Mistakes were inevitable but one I regret involved Jim Smith.

At a press conference I had called I stated that I had to improve the fitness levels of the players. It seemed to me to be an innocent and valid statement.

Not long after, I called Jim at Newcastle to see how he had settled in at St James' Park and sensed that this was not the usual Jim Smith. He seemed unhappy. I asked him if something was wrong and he told me he was disappointed about my comments regarding fitness levels as he saw it as a criticism of him.

I was mortified as that was never my intention and I apologised profusely.

Jim accepted my apology and our good relationship was immediately restored.

What working under Graeme had not exposed me to was the strange ways of the football club owner and/ or chairman. As you will read in the remaining chapters of my book I have had my fair share of them and I did not have to wait long for my first odd experience.

In a meeting not long after he had appointed me as his player-manager, Richard Thompson, the chairman at QPR, declared unashamedly to me that he was a Tottenham Hotspur supporter.

Not particularly strange you are thinking, but then the conversation moved on. Richard told me that the penultimate home game of the season was against his beloved Tottenham Hotspur. The conversation continued that as long as Rangers were clear of any relegation fears could I name him as one of our substitutes for the Spurs match? That was a bizarre enough request but then he topped it by telling me that I could bring him on for the last 20 minutes! I started laughing until I realised he was serious!

At the age of 26 he was the youngest chairman in the league and therefore perhaps a little naïve to ask for such an impossible favour. As the youngest manager in the league I knew it could never happen.

It was 18 January 1989 and we were drawn away to Nottingham Forest in the quarter-final of the Littlewoods Cup. We lost the game 5-2 at the City Ground and a handful of Forest fans invaded the pitch much to the dismay of Brian Clough, who regarded his pitch as his working domain. So disgusted was he that he went on to the pitch and physically attacked some of the intruders.

It should have been Lee Chapman, who scored four goals on the night, who made the headlines but, as was often the case, it was Clough who hogged the front and back pages for days to come.

Clough claimed that he just wanted to help the police clear the pitch as quickly as possible but the FA thought otherwise and issued a £5,000 fine and a touchline ban for the remainder of the season.

At the post-match press conference I was asked for my thoughts on Brian Clough hitting the supporters to which I replied, 'I just wish he had hit a couple of my players!'

When I was at Queens Park Rangers I was aware that we had a young 22-year-old player out on loan in Turkey playing for Besiktas JK. The manager of Besiktas JK at the time was Gordon Milne, who I had come across on two previous occasions: as part-time manager of the England Under-18s and as manager of Coventry City when I left Birmingham City for Nottingham Forest.

I was looking for a big, strong centre-forward with pace and this loanee seemed to fit the bill. So I contacted Gordon and he said the lad was doing well and enjoying life in Turkey, and instead of Gordon sending him back to London he offered £100,000 as his transfer fee from Queens Park Rangers.

Obviously this surprised me slightly but as manager I had to bring the offer to the attention of our chairman. Richard did not dismiss the offer out of hand and indeed was in two minds as to whether to take the money or not.

I asked him not to take the £100,000 and let me get the player back to Loftus Road so that I could work with him and make him a better player who would have a much higher valuation than had been offered.

The chairman supported me and the legendary Les Ferdinand came back to England, and the rest as they say is history as he went on to have a great career.

Les left QPR in 1995 to join Newcastle United for £6 million having scored 80 goals for the Hoops, averaging a goal every two games.

Just think of that – Les Ferdinand could have been lost to Turkish football without my intervention.

One of my best days playing for the Hoops was as a 35-year-old playing against Graham Taylor's Aston Villa at Villa Park.

Of course, as an ex-Birmingham City player playing against the Villa evoked a lot of memories of those torrid derby games. At the time Villa were going well and were second in the league. They took the lead through David Platt and there was a feeling amongst the Villa fans that that was it – game over. That was never my mentality and the history books show that I responded with a hat-trick. My third goal involved me lobbing their goalkeeper from the edge of the penalty box. As you can imagine, that hat-trick goal was not well received by the Villa fans. The response from the away end of the ground was abnormally vocal, from what seemed to be the largest away following QPR had had that season.

After the game, the reason for the large away following was explained. The planned away Birmingham City fixture had been cancelled early enough in the day for a couple of thousand disappointed Birmingham City supporters to move across the city to support QPR and me. The away end was a mass of blue and white scarves (no replica shirts in those days) and of course there was no telling whether they were fans of Birmingham City or Queens Park Rangers.

Having scored my three goals I decided to gain the best possible reaction from the fans in the away end. I chose to substitute myself and took as slow a walk off the pitch as the referee would allow. The Villa fans, not surprisingly, reacted badly and the hostility I felt was immense. But this was my moment and as an adopted Brummie I was determined to enjoy it.

One of the questions I am often asked which I find difficult to answer is, 'What do you consider to be your best achievement as a player? Scoring four goals as a 16-year-old or three as a 35-year-old?'

I have to consider that the four goals as a 16-year-old were scored in Division Two whilst the three as a 35-year-old were in the top league and I was a player-manager! What do you think?

On the subject of hat-tricks, I scored six in England including four for Birmingham City against Bolton Wanderers, Luton Town, Arsenal and Bristol City. Aside from the four goals when I was 16, the other hat-trick was against Manchester City for Nottingham Forest.

I attempted to change things and bring in methods I had learnt from my days in Italy, such as better diets and training methods. Away from the training pitch, one of my initiatives off the pitch was to re-establish the supporters' club, which was greatly appreciated by the fans. I also wanted to involve the fans in players' events – one which comes to mind was a cricket match in which the club fielded a team against Shepherds Bush Cricket Club – funnily enough I can't remember the score.

In retrospect I believe that I tried to change too many things too quickly and undoubtedly that led to my downfall and contributed to my hasty departure from Loftus Road.

The impact of a good diet on a player's performance had been evidenced during my time in Italy and therefore I felt that changing the players' eating habits would have a positive effect on our results. Previously on away trips the players would stop off and get fish and chips. For me, that had to stop so it became a routine for the kit man to go to a supermarket the day before we travelled to buy salads, pasta and fruit. I made this decision firmly in the belief that this would be more beneficial to the team. The new regime did not go down well with the players – but this was in 1988.

I remember the *London Evening Standard* doing a major article on my managerial methods. There I was being ridiculed by the London media for making my players eat pasta! Think about that? In today's football world you would be ridiculed if the players did not eat pasta! It only proves the point that in the 80s European football was well ahead of England in terms of pre-match preparation.

At Queens Park Rangers I was sorry to be part of what became a notorious event involving one of my players, Martin Allen. It all happened on 11 March 1989.

It is not something I look back on with any fond memories, bearing in mind that I am very much a family man and was present at the birth of my first son, Matthew, in 1979.

When I went to play my football in Italy the professionalism of the players compared to what I was leaving behind in England was a real eye-opener. It was very noticeable that whenever a player's wife was about to have a baby there was never any suggestion that, if it interfered with matchdays, the player would miss the game – it was unthinkable! If the baby was being born on a Sunday afternoon (the Italian matchday) then the player played!

Remember that Queens Park Rangers was my first managerial role and basically I took a lot of the things that I had learnt in Italy into my style of management.

I recall that Martin Allen's wife was very close to giving birth and we were due to leave on the Friday to go to Newcastle. I spoke with him prior to travelling to get a full update: What were his thoughts? Was he thinking of not going? He was positive that he wanted to be there, so he travelled with the team. As far as I was concerned that was the end of the matter. I had spoken to the player about his personal circumstances and he had made a decision, a decision I had accepted when thinking about team selection for the forthcoming game.

On the Saturday morning I received a telephone call from our physio saying that during the night Martin had had a call to say that his wife had gone into labour. He had left the hotel and returned to London. I took a dim view because he had put himself up to play and then left the team. I fined him for leaving the team's headquarters without permission. In my mind you have to deal with individual situations like this with a view to what message it gives to the rest of the squad. I had to try to prevent such a situation happening again with another player. I can reflect on it now but it caused me so much embarrassment at the time. I never expected such a negative reaction.

For me, although I was new to management, I had taken the actions that I thought to be correct.

After the baby arrived I personally sent a bouquet of flowers, congratulating them on the birth of their child.

My action really divided opinion – the furore created by my decision to fine him was amazing. It was even discussed in the Houses of Parliament!

The media were full of it and I was labelled everything you could possibly think of – 'cruel' being the one I remember because that hurt me.

It is easy with hindsight to feel that mistakes were made. I should never have taken him to Newcastle. Having decided to take him I should have given greater consideration to the rooming arrangements – he was rooming with our goalkeeper David Seaman who was kept awake all night by what happened. Hardly ideal preparation.

All you can do is learn from your mistakes and, to that end, I acted differently when the same situation presented itself later in my career.

It was great material for the newspaper reporters who jumped on it. I remember going to Sandy Lyle's Masters golf victory party at his home and when speaking with Sandy, Nick Faldo and Ronan Rafferty, the incident cropped up. Their view was if the baby had been due on the last day of a major golf tournament then they would still have to play; what was the problem? Everyone had a point of view: a long-haul pilot made the point that if he was halfway through a journey he would have no option but to carry on flying – he had to do so. Having said that there were also hundreds and hundreds who were pro-Martin Allen. All I can say is that I did what I thought was right. It's not a subject I particularly relish talking about as I was made out to be some kind of a monster.

As a footnote I was playing in Italy when my second son was born. Helen flew back to England where it was arranged that the baby would be induced on the Monday. This gave me the opportunity to play football on the Sunday and fly back on the Monday morning to see James born. I highly recommend being present at the birth of your child – it is wonderful to see. Now that is a big story!

Chapter Nine
Sheffield Wednesday FC

As player and player-manager: 38 senior
appearances, 51 substitute appearances; 9 goals

WHEN I was sacked from Queens Park Rangers I felt my whole world was falling apart, as this was the first time I had experienced being sacked. It wasn't a nice feeling and I remember driving home to my wife in tears. There were lots of people from the game who called me in an effort to console me as well as giving me their best wishes.

Then Ron Atkinson called. No time was wasted on sympathy, he just said, 'Get yourself up to Sheffield Wednesday.' He talked about Sheffield being like Rome with its six hills. Ron always had a romantic nature!

Looking back it was just what I needed to prevent me from feeling too sorry for myself. So I went up to Hillsborough and linked up with Ron for the first time after a number of missed opportunities in the past. Playing under Ron was like a breath of fresh air. He was great, a player's type of manager. No one who has played for Ron has a bad word to say about him because he was just great to play for. I soon realised that Sheffield is a great footballing city and the size of Sheffield Wednesday made it, in my mind, a big club.

My first goal for Sheffield Wednesday was against Bristol Rovers away from home. The Rovers did not have their own ground and had a temporary home at Twerton Park.

It only had a capacity of around 6,000 and the stands were makeshift affairs. As it was, it was packed with Sheffield Wednesday fans including Helen, James and Matthew. My boys were only three and ten respectively and the stand was nothing more than a shed.

When I scored the fans surged forward on to the track surrounding the playing area and then on to the pitch. It was pure excitement and nothing untoward happened.

Unfortunately the police got involved and they decided to escort the Wednesday fans out of the ground much to my dismay, as they included Helen and the boys.

There was nothing I could do as I was on the pitch. I felt so helpless.

Helen took the boys back to our car until the game was over.

At least they got to see me score my first goal for the Owls.

Little did I know that eventually I would be managing the club!

In my first season, 1989/90, we were relegated and Ron talked about resigning. But I and a few other players managed to talk him into staying. The following season was a very successful one because we got promotion and won the League Cup, beating Manchester United in the final with me a non-playing substitute.

At the end of that season it was a huge disappointment for everyone at the club when Ron moved to Aston Villa. I think he advised the board to give me the job and I was very happy to accept the offer to become Sheffield Wednesday's first, and to date only, player-manager, on 18 June 1991. This was the second time in my career that I took on the role of player-manager. It's a very difficult job combining the two roles but at the time it was very fashionable and it was something a lot of players tried with probably Kenny Dalglish being the most successful.

I recognised that this was a big opportunity for me. Many in the game felt that this was an opportunity that I could not mess up and I didn't disagree with that assessment. My thought process had changed from my days at Queens Park Rangers. I had seen for 18 months how Ron Atkinson worked and, whilst as characters we were chalk and cheese (thinking about it there are not too many people like Ron), I liked his management methods. I knew what the players wanted and how they responded to the type of training that was instigated by Ron. I made my mind up that I wanted that to continue. This was a little against my natural tendency but I was following a man with vast experience. I was a novice in management compared to Ron Atkinson. I added to the squad by bringing in the likes of Chris Woods, which at £1.2m broke the British transfer record for a goalkeeper, and Paul Warhurst, who was a very versatile defender who I later transformed into a very effective centre-forward.

That first season as Wednesday's player-manager was a very good one and for a long time we were in with a shout of winning the title although we never talked about it. All the talk was about Manchester United and Leeds United in both the press and on the terraces. In the end we finished third in the top division, with Leeds as champions. Leeds United were managed by Howard Wilkinson, who is a good friend of mine. It might surprise some readers to know that he was the last Englishman to win the league!

During my first season at Sheffield Wednesday Helen and I had stayed at a hotel just outside the city. Carlton Palmer and his wife were also staying there.

One Friday night in August 1991, before our game against Queens Park Rangers, there was a problem at the hotel.

The chef had walked out and the kitchen was closed. This created a problem for us as we needed to eat as part of our preparation for the following day.

Fortunately we had a good relationship with the hotel management which enabled Helen to ask whether she could prepare a pasta dish for us both. The manager agreed.

Understandably Carlton asked if he could join us, to which Helen agreed but said, 'That's fine but in return I want a goal from you against QPR because they sacked my husband.'

Well, there must have been something in the pasta or was it Helen's management style because at half-time we were 3-0 up due to a hat-trick from Carlton, and not surprisingly we went on to win the game – 4-1. Carlton Palmer had won it for us, which was made even more amazing by the fact that he only scored five all that season! Throughout his career of close to 600 games he only scored 32, a strike rate of a goal in every 18 matches.

What was even more incredible was that Carlton had a terrible reputation for his shooting ability. When Ron Atkinson was manager and Carlton got anywhere near the goal, he would shout to the nearest Wednesday player, 'Tackle him, don't let him shoot!'

Sheffield Wednesday had qualified for the UEFA Cup.

In July 1992 I paid £1m to Marseille for Chris Waddle. I negotiated the transfer in Paris with Marseille's president, Bernard Tapie. My board of directors was reluctant to pay his salary of £200,000 but it turned out to be money well spent.

Chris added so much to our team. He was simply brilliant. That first season he was the catalyst that got us to two cup finals (League and FA) against Arsenal. He was rightly named the Football Writers' Association Footballer of the Year and became the first Sheffield Wednesday player to win this accolade. He was playing so well that in my opinion he should have won a recall to the England team. That didn't happen but I think you would be hard-pushed to find a Wednesday fan who would not say he was the greatest player ever seen at Hillsborough.

In both games against Arsenal it was difficult to impose ourselves because of the smothering tactics employed by George Graham. We played our normal game as a very expansive team playing 4-4-2, with plenty of width to our game. Arsenal were tough and resolute defensively and closed the spaces down very quickly.

In that season we were at Wembley four times in four weeks. The first was the semi-final of the FA Cup, a game we had to win because it was against Sheffield United! We did win but lost the League Cup Final. The FA Cup Final went to a replay on a Thursday night which we lost in extra time with 30 seconds to go.

Heartbreak, but they were great days and when I look back with the Wednesday fans at some of the players we had at the club, not all at the same time, obviously, but consider the likes of Chris Woods, Carlton Palmer, Andy Sinton, Des Walker, Chris Waddle and David Hirst – all England internationals who gave us some great memories!

As a founder member of the Premier League, after BSkyB paid £304m for the broadcasting rights, I needed to improve the team to make sure we benefitted financially from our final position. But doing that made it more and more difficult to find a place in the line-up for myself.

Placing the club ahead of any personal ambitions meant I failed to achieve my desire to play at the age of 40. I was 39 when I retired and I often think that I could have played at 40, but the bloody manager would not select me!

After that we finished seventh and then the next season we got to the semi-final of the League Cup and finished seventh again. The fourth season was a more difficult one and we finished 13th. I was dismissed. The pressures of managing in the Premier League had started on day one and it was difficult to replace players like Palmer and Pearson because on occasions their replacements turned out not to be of the required standard.

In 1992, whilst we were still finding our feet in the top division, I got a call from Dennis Roach, the agent who had taken me from Manchester City to Sampdoria. He wanted me to do him a favour on behalf of Michel Platini who was the French team manager at the time.

Dennis was asking me whether I would allow Eric Cantona, who was coming out of retirement, to train with us for a few days.

Before agreeing I told Dennis that I didn't mind helping as long as it did not cost the club any money – air fares, hotels, other travel – everything had to be paid for by his party. It was all agreed and Eric arrived for two days' training. Unfortunately it was in a period when it was very wintry in Sheffield, such that we could not get on the training field. On the first day of Eric's stay we had to use an AstroTurf pitch in Rotherham and on the second we played an indoor game against an American team.

Cantona played quite well in that game and there was a lobby from the media about Wednesday signing him. There was never, ever any suggestion of us signing Eric Cantona. He was there purely as a favour for Dennis Roach and Platini. I had made that clear right from the start. The only proactive thing that came from me was to say that I would like him to stay for another day because it would be good to see him train on grass.

Eric was accompanied by a huge entourage including press officer, agent and personal manager. Somehow they had translated my suggestion for a further day's training into my wanting him on trial. Therefore it was no surprise when word got back to me that Eric Cantona was not here on trial. I knew that; it wasn't about a trial.

At that time Howard Wilkinson, the Leeds United manager, spoke to Eric's advisers, who announced that they had an offer for him to go to Leeds. I was more than happy for him to do so. And that was the story. Even today, and it's partly my fault because I have never before explained the full story, people still ask, 'How did you miss out on Eric Cantona? How come you never signed him?'

Without going into too much detail one of the reasons would have been that I already had my players in forward areas but having said that you can never have too many forward players in my opinion. The kind of contract he would have wanted would have killed my whole budget as we were a team that had just come out of the second division.

Hopefully this puts to bed the Cantona story – another myth!

It was a night match at Goodison Park in 1993 when in amongst the large contingent of Sheffield Wednesday fans I heard for the first time the unusual sound of bugles being blown.

There were three or four people blowing their bugles and it generated a good atmosphere to which the fans responded.

When I was back home I contacted the producer of the local radio programme *Praise and Grumble* and asked if anyone knew the answer to the question, 'Who is the leader of the buglers?'

Shortly afterwards I received a call at my office in Hillsborough and was told that the band leader was John Hemingway. I arranged to meet him as I wanted the band of buglers to play regularly at our games. John told me that he had to smuggle in his instrument under his jumper. I told him about my idea for a regular band as I had experienced similar in-crowd entertainment whilst in Italy. John agreed to my suggestion and I said I would see if the club would pay for other instruments to accompany the buglers.

I spoke with my chairman Dave Richards and he was pleased to announce to the fans that the club would pay for drums and other instruments and the Wednesday Kop Band was born.

They have now been playing at every home and away game for a quarter of a century, with various members. Some are regarded as mainstays but the group also encourages guest appearances; some band members have hung up their instruments after years of service.

In 1996 the band began to play at England matches.

It was at a game between Wednesday and Arsenal at Highbury in 1993 that the idea of an England band was touted. Impressed by the noise and atmosphere the band created amongst the away fans during a 4-1 defeat to the Gunners, the watching England manager Glenn Hoddle and FA chief executive David Davies were keen to start something similar for the national team.

Davies asked Sheffield Wednesday for their contact details and the band made their international debut against Poland at Wembley in October 1996. England won the game 2-1.

It makes you wonder what the season ticket holder that sits next to John Hemingway feels when the band begins to play!

It was 1993 when we got to the two cup finals and it coincided with a period when we had as many as five strikers injured at the same time. I was aware at the start of the week that none of these players would be available for the Saturday.

I looked at the squad and then had a word with Paul Warhurst, who I had brought to the club from Oldham Athletic when I first joined. He was quite a versatile central defender or full-back, with great pace, which I have always admired as a great attribute.

In my office on the Monday morning I asked Paul, 'Have you ever played as a striker?' to which he replied, 'Never.' So I told him my thinking: he'd got great pace and we needed someone up front who could get behind and stretch defenders. I told him I would work with him all week on the training pitch if he was prepared to give it a go ready for Saturday.

We trained normally, then had an 11 v 11 game only for 20 minutes and he was very impressive. We did the same the following day and I showed him one or two runs he could make. He scored a couple of goals and I had no hesitation in playing him on the Saturday.

He was very good and he played such a big part as a striker in helping us get to the finals that he eventually got called up to the England squad.

We lost the first final at Wembley against Arsenal when Paul played up front. By the time the second final came around the injury situation had eased and I had my recognised front two available – David Hirst and Mark Bright. At the same time I had injury problems in the heart of my defence. On the day before the second final we were at Bisham Abbey as we had stayed over in Windsor. All week I was looking at the defensive situation and the players I was considering did not make it. So that Friday morning, without naming the team, I gave the squad a very good idea of what I was going to do by doing a little bit of team shaping with the players I was planning to use on the Saturday. I stopped and started the play often, to let them defend set pieces and then attack set pieces, switching in a short space of time which is something I like to do. I do not like to go into games without the players having an idea of what will be the format of the team. So I gave the bibs out and I decided that Paul would play as a central defender – when I gave him the bib he refused to play there saying, 'I'm a striker.' I replied that I had a lot of defensive problems and I wanted him to play as a central defender and he again refused saying, 'I'm not doing it.' I said, 'So you are saying to me that you are refusing to play in a cup final tomorrow?'

I was put in a difficult position because there I was on the training pitch and the other players could see what was happening. I really should not have put myself in that position but I never expected that sort of response and I don't mind admitting it, it was a very difficult moment. Fortunately, in the squad I had some senior, experienced players who recognised what was happening and they got hold of Paul and more or less said to him in no uncertain terms, 'What are you playing at, you are playing tomorrow.' Thank goodness he put the bib on and agreed to play.

Soon after I bought Des Walker from Sampdoria. Everyone knew Des was a class player having played for Nottingham Forest and England, but I did not realise that he disliked training as much as he did.

He continued to live in Nottingham and, against my wishes and club policy, travelled up to Sheffield for training. Whenever I did work with the back four and midfield four he rarely applied himself fully. This became a hindrance and the other players were getting agitated by the whole thing. They wanted to work but Des did not want to do any of the preparation work I was trying to implement.

So after a while I made the decision that as Des was a naturally fit boy he could come in on a Monday and then stay in Nottingham for the rest of the week because he was not helping the sessions with his clear dislike of working. He would then come back up on Friday in preparation for Saturday's game.

To be fair to him in match situations he always gave absolutely his best and he was a good player for me but not a good trainer, and it was fortunate for us all that he had high natural fitness levels.

It never happened with any other player and if it had happened in my early days at QPR then clearly I would have handled the situation very differently. You learn in management and you learn from other managers.

When I made that decision it was very much with Ron Atkinson in mind because it was something that he would have done. As important as training is, you are judged as a manager by the way the team plays and ultimately it is all about getting points.

Our best striker at Sheffield Wednesday was undoubtedly David Hirst but like me he was blighted by injury so we never saw the best of him because he was constantly in and out of the treatment room. When he was fit he was a very good player. I remember seeing his debut for England on the same night as Alan Shearer made his debut and there was very little to choose between the two of them.

Manchester United were following David for a while when Alex Ferguson was manager and I can still hear Alex now on my car phone totally exasperated with me because he had put in two offers which I had knocked back. He then offered £4m and with the 100 per cent backing of the board I told him we were not interested in doing anything with David Hirst. I refused £4m and Alex bellowed down the phone in his Scottish accent, 'Do you realise this is Manchester United Football Club and you are stopping a player from going to Man Utd?' I told him that Sheffield Wednesday were a big club, not as big as Man Utd, and that I was looking to continue the improvements I was making and David Hirst was a big part of my plans. I stuck to my guns but I will never forget Alex Ferguson telling me what he thought of me! I was on the M1 motorway and he was not aware that Helen was in the car listening to him on the speaker phone. If she had been a referee he would undoubtedly have been given a red card for his bad language!

I was backed by the board over the David Hirst business but little did we know that another opportunity was soon going to require their approval.

When I was at Sheffield Wednesday we had Hirst, Bright and Nigel Jemson as striking options. I watched Alan Shearer playing for Southampton and have never been more certain about a player, bearing in mind that when you are considering any player you can never be 100 per cent sure about how it will turn out. I was never more certain about a player than I was about Alan Shearer.

I remember at the time I rang Alan to ask him if he would be interested in coming to Sheffield Wednesday. The fee was £3m. I went to our chairman, Dave Richards, and said, 'Listen, it's a lot of money but I have never been more certain about a player – I guarantee that in a couple of years' time, if you wanted to, you would be able to double your money.' We did not sign him and he went to Blackburn Rovers for around £4m in 1996 and then, after helping Rovers win the Premiership, went to Newcastle United for an enormous fee of well over £15m.

Whilst there was no interest from the Wednesday board, my business partner at the time, property developer Nick Rogers, who was not a football man, said, 'Between us can't we buy him?' I told him that the rules meant that you could not do that in English football.

I remember Carlos Tevez at West Ham United being owned by a third party but in 1993 that was not an option.

The situation with a normal transfer is that the player's registration passes from the seller to the buying club for a pre-agreed fee. An agent can be employed by the player or either club (but not more than one party) to negotiate the deal. The club and the player come to an agreement on who retains the player's commercial rights. The situation with Tevez was that his commercial rights were owned by two companies, Media Sports Investments Ltd and Just Sports Inc, who loaned his registration to West Ham. West Ham were fined £5.5m because this was against Premier League rules.

In August 1992 before a home game against Nottingham Forest their team bus pulled up at Hillsborough and word got back to me that Brian Clough had got off the bus and was the worse for drink!

That was later confirmed when at 2.20pm, with the players out warming up, one of our apprentices knocked on my door and said that Mr Clough had asked for two buckets of water. I told him if he'd asked for them to take them in. A couple of minutes later the same apprentice knocked on my door saying Mr Clough had asked the apprentice to pour the buckets of water over his head. I told him if he'd asked for that then to do it.

We kicked off at 3pm and with 20 minutes to go we were leading 2-0. The referee blew for an infringement. Brian Clough came out of the dugout, came over to me, shook my hand and said, 'Young man, your team played well and were the better team today.'

I said, 'Boss, the game hasn't finished yet!'

That was Brian Clough's last season at Forest.

It's been said that when players cross the white line at 2.55pm there is nothing a manager can do.

I have never understood that saying as in my opinion there is a whole host of things a manager can do – check that the opposition is set up as we planned it before kick-off, tweak things in the hope of improving the chances of getting a good result, change the shape of the team or move players into different roles to exploit an opponent's weakness or negate the opposition's threat.

Later in the game there is of course the tactical use of substitutions.

So I believe there is plenty that a manager can do to influence the result of a game once it has started.

The routine on a matchday is to hand in the team sheet at 2pm and then five minutes later put the opposing team's line-up on the board in the home dressing room.

For a manager the period between 2.15pm and 2.45pm is when you are looking for something to do.

There are two potential options: either stay in the dressing room with the players or, if at home, invite the opposition manager into your office for a drink – normally a cup of tea.

Once, at Sheffield Wednesday, when we were at home to Everton who were managed at the time by Howard Kendall, I invited Howard to join me for a cup of tea or coffee as we knew each other well from our days at Birmingham City and were keen to reminisce about old times.

Howard accepted my offer of a drink but asked if I had something stronger than tea or coffee.

I found a bottle of Chablis and poured a glass for Howard and one for myself, which is something I rarely do. But I felt that as we went back some way I should keep Howard company.

Soon, after another drink, I realised it was 2.45pm and I said to Howard, 'I've got to go as it is 15 minutes to kick-off.'

Howard replied, 'Leave the bottle here.'

I went to the dressing room and spent a few minutes with the players before taking my place in the directors' box where I preferred to watch the game at the start of proceedings.

That was the first and last time I drank alcohol before a game. Why? Because I did not feel as alert as I wanted to be; in fact I felt a little sleepy!

Chapter Ten

England

DON REVIE was appointed England team manager in July 1974 and immediately arranged a get-together in Manchester for established and potential England players. We gathered at the hotel on the Saturday evening for the meeting on the Sunday (no Sunday fixtures in those days). As well as trying to make everyone feel part of the new set-up he announced that he would get extra pay for international players and bonuses for wins and draws. A total of 81 players were there but only 34 went on to win caps under Revie, which, if my maths is right, means that 47 of those players in Manchester that weekend never played for England.

Newspaper headlines for the next few days were all about who had been omitted rather than those who had made the final squad. What that get-together demonstrated was the incredible competition there was for every position.

Because of the influx of foreign players into the English league there is nowhere near the number of options there are today for the England manager to consider. Does that make it easier for the manager? Probably not. Complacency was never an option in 1974: you felt you had to play at the top of your game, every game to keep your place in the team.

It wasn't until 1982 that I felt confident about playing regularly for England, which was five years after my debut. The competition was fierce. In the early days of Don Revie's reign I was competing with the likes of Mick Channon, Charlie George, Kevin Keegan, Bob Latchford, Stuart Pearson, Stan Bowles, Allan Clarke, David Johnson, Malcolm Macdonald and John Richards.

It was 1974 when I was tipped off by the London press that I would be making my England debut on the Wednesday after a league game away at Sheffield United on the Saturday. Unfortunately I got injured and had to wait another three years before my dream could come true and I could play for England.

I viewed every game for England, whether it was a friendly or a World Cup game, as a big occasion. To score in only my second appearance was another career highlight.

My full international career was delayed due to injury but I still made my debut at the age of 22 years and 296 days in 1977. Between October 1974 and November 1976 I missed out on 22 potential England caps.

Injuries blighted my England career even to the extent of not playing in the 1980 European Championships – a once in a lifetime experience I never had.

As part of the process of writing this book I wanted to find out what my potential number of England appearances would have been had I not been injured. Here goes:

I made 52 appearances.

During the period June 1978 to May 1979 I was out for 12 months which meant I missed seven internationals. From April 1980 to February 1981 I had another year out of action, missing 11 internationals. In the period October 1983 to March 1984 I missed three internationals due to a seven-month lay-off. I was unavailable for six internationals in the ten months between July 1985 and March 1986. Add in the 22 internationals between 1974 and 1976 and the total is 49 missed opportunities to wear an England shirt.

Although I enjoyed playing for England immensely I am sure you can share my frustration at injuries causing me to miss so many international games. It causes me even greater sadness when I realise that those 'missed' games together with my actual games would have given me the chance to join the 'century club'! My potential haul could have been 101 caps – what an achievement that would have been!

I appreciate that many players think that they should have played more times for their country but for me I think it's different as I can evidence the missed opportunities.

Looking at both sides of the situation I must also remember that a back injury to Kevin Keegan enabled me to play in all the games in the 1982 World Cup. Would I have played if Kevin had been fit?

For the 1982 World Cup in Spain we were based in Bilbao and drawn against France, Czechoslovakia and Kuwait in Group 4. In the opening game Bryan Robson scored what was at the time the quickest goal in World Cup history – after 27 seconds in our 3-1 win over France.

We topped our group and went on to the second round of the competition, playing West Germany and Spain in Group B. This was the last World Cup tournament with two group leagues, as from 1986 the format went to its existing group stage followed by knockout matches. This was the only time this format was used – how unlucky was that for England? The format meant that we had played five games and had not lost one, drawing two and winning three. Had the format been different, who knows?

In Group B we finished second to West Germany after drawing 0-0 with Spain. There was a lot of hostility towards England both inside and outside of the Bernabeu stadium due to the Falkland Islands conflict. Indeed, our participation in the tournament was only confirmed days before the World Cup finals started. Spain were supporters of Argentina.

It was a tradition back in the 70s and 80s that England World Cup squads made a record and the 1982 squad was no different.

We recorded a song entitled 'This Time (We'll Get It Right)' which got to number two in the UK charts and resulted in the squad performing 'live' on the iconic television programme, Top Of The Pops.

The song was written by two members of the pop group Smokie, who also wrote the 'B' side which was entitled 'England – We'll Fly the Flag'.

As was often the case in those days, any recording artist that had a hit single was required to record an album.

Viv Anderson and I were called to the famous Abbey Road recording studios to perform our track for the album.

For some reason, two Nottingham Forest players were being asked to sing the Liverpool anthem 'You'll Never Walk Alone'.

This song proved too difficult for Viv and myself and after several takes it was decided to jettison the idea of us singing the classic ballad. At the time Telly Savalas, who played the title role in Kojak, had had a big hit with a song by Bread called 'If' in which he talked through the lyrics, making no attempt to find a tune.

It was decided, much to the relief of Viv and myself, that we would do exactly the same and surprisingly it made the finished album.

Keegan and Trevor Brooking missed almost the whole tournament due to injury and were only declared fit to sit on the bench for the Spain game. They both came on as substitutes in the 63rd minute, for Woodcock and Rix respectively, much to the disappointment of Keegan. My

Me at 16 in 1970 – nickname 'Superboy'

Jim Smith – the Birmingham City manager who set my £1m price tag

George Best and me in Detroit

Franz Beckenbauer – still friends after my six goals against him

Alan Ball, Johnny Giles and me in Detroit

In the boss's office shortly after signing for Forest

Helen and I after Forest signing

In action for Forest

Malmo goal – the most important goal in my career

Peter Shilton and I with the European Cup

Pitch celebrations after Malmo win

Me with the European Cup on my head

Mister Blue Sky – Jeff Lynne of The Electric Light Orchestra with me and the European Cup

Hairy Bikers – Tony Woodcock and I

With Sir Alf Ramsey as part of the England Under 23 team

Liam Brady and I relaxing at the Sampdoria training ground

Graeme Souness and me with the Scottish pipers in Italy

Zico and I

international career certainly had its highlights: scoring twice against Denmark in Bobby Robson's first game as England manager was one of them.

When I made my debut, Keegan, Stan Bowles and I were the three strikers. We were sent out by Revie without any tactics or attacking practice; it was very much a matter of play your normal club game.

Just for the record, the England team for my debut was: Ray Clemence – Dave Clement – Kevin Beattie – Dave Watson – Mike Doyle – Paul Madeley (Stuart Pearson, 74) – Kevin Keegan (captain) – Brian Greenhoff (Colin Todd, 40) – me – Stan Bowles and Trevor Brooking.

After achieving my first international objective of playing at Wembley for England it did not take long before I achieved my second ambition, which was to play at the Maracana stadium in Rio de Janeiro, Brazil.

The game against Brazil was the first of a three-match friendly end-of-season tour which also included matches against Argentina and Uruguay.

I played well in the goalless draw with Brazil which regrettably the manager, Don Revie, did not see as I believe he was away in the Middle East negotiating a lucrative contract to manage the United Arab Emirates national team.

For whatever reason I was not selected for the Argentina game on 12 June 1977, which was to be played at the home of Boca Juniors in Buenos Aires.

The 1-1 draw was played in the most intimidating atmosphere I have experienced from the bench – just as hostile as the matches between Rangers and Celtic. The home crowd were venting their anger at Sir Alf Ramsey's comments in the 1966 World Cup tournament, when he called the Argentinians 'animals'. Imagine still being angry and insulted by something which happened 11 years before.

However, it was not just the crowd – the home players were equally aggressive and punch-ups were occurring throughout the game, one of which involved my room-mate, Trevor Cherry of Leeds United, who was in a scuffle with Daniel Bertoni which resulted in them both being sent off.

I did not see much of Trevor that night as he was in hospital after losing a tooth.

* * *

In June 1985 I played in the two games in Mexico, against Italy and Mexico, planned as a dress rehearsal for the 1986 World Cup in Mexico.

Bobby Robson came over to Italy to watch me play on a number of occasions and we developed a good relationship off the field. I remember him once playing Lego with my seven-year-old son, Matthew, on the floor of our home prior to us taking him out for dinner. I felt we had a good relationship but that later proved not to be the case.

In April 1986 we were due to play Scotland before Bobby announced his squad of 23 for the World Cup. On the Sunday before the players met up the next day, I was playing for Sampdoria, damaged my face and was in a lot of pain. Once I was in England I was sent straight to a local hospital for X-rays where the specialist confirmed that I had fractured my cheekbone. I asked the doctor whether I would be able to play in my condition. He was indecisive and would not tell me not to play or give me the all-clear.

This left me with a dilemma as the decision as to whether I played rested with me. Before I could make my decision I needed the answer to a very important question.

I went to see Bobby the day before the game and explained my predicament. I did not think my request for a private meeting was unreasonable. I was 32 years of age, a senior player and had won 51 caps. I was both surprised and disappointed by his reaction.

He was very uncomfortable and was unable to give me a definitive answer. As a friend and my manager, with whom I had had a long and trusting relationship, I expected him to allow me into his thought process regarding the forthcoming World Cup.

With no directive from Bobby there was only one conclusion I could come to which was to declare myself fit to play against Scotland, even though their central defenders were the no-nonsense pairing of Willie Miller and Alex McLeish. I played, and we won 2-1. After the game I went straight to Watford for an operation on my face the following morning.

The same day I got hold of a copy of the *London Evening Standard* and there in black and white print was the England squad minus my name. I felt let down.

For Bobby not to have taken the time to inform me personally of his decision clearly demonstrated that the good relationship I thought we had was very much one-sided. I never broached the subject with him but I ensured through an 'exclusive' in *The Sun* that he knew how shabbily I felt I had been treated. I was not proud of my action in talking to the journalist but I felt the need to tell my story. It was a sad way to end my England career.

Looking back, my debut against Holland at Wembley in 1977 was a wonderful occasion. I was greatly supported by the thousands of Birmingham City fans who came down the M1 to London to watch my first game in an England shirt. Although we lost the game it was a wonderful experience to play against the great Johan Cruyff.

Naturally I was very nervous as it was such a huge occasion but I was told to go out and achieve a minimum of 75 per cent of my normal club form, which wasn't that easy to do. As well as getting instructions about how to play we were also given other instructions – for example about swapping shirts with the opponents. It wasn't like today's game when you could change shirts at half-time. You only had one shirt and you weren't allowed to be seen swapping shirts on the field. If you wanted to swap shirts you had to wait until you were in the tunnel, as dictated by an FA handbook of 'dos and don'ts'. As I came off, feeling proud, even though we had lost the match 2-0, there was a little tap on my shoulder and this guy wanted to change shirts with me. I could not believe that it was the great man Johan Cruyff. Imagine me refusing to swap shirts with Johan Cruyff! But that's what I did because the shirt symbolised the achievement of my dream to play for my country and I thought, 'this could be the only England shirt I will ever get'.

My career lasted nine years and 73 days of which I am very proud.

Three significant managers thought I was worth a place in the England set-up: Ron Greenwood, Bobby Robson and Don Revie. Fortunately I was able to score for all of them, once for Revie in four matches, four goals for Robson in 20 matches and seven for Greenwood in 28 games.

I scored goals against Luxembourg, Hungary, Northern Ireland, Spain, Wales, Czechoslovakia, Kuwait, Denmark and Australia, against whom I also earned a yellow card.

The yellow card was given to me for an innocuous trip which, considering the treatment I had received during the three Australian fixtures, was ironic – at times I felt I was playing Australian rules football. Then, in the 73rd minute, we were awarded a penalty. I took it and scored, sending the goalkeeper the wrong way. Imagine my surprise when the referee Jack Johnson announced that he had disallowed the goal because he had not blown the whistle to signal that the kick could be taken. Unfortunately I blasted the retake over the bar.

* * *

During my career I was lucky enough to play alongside some icons of English football. I played 40 times with the late Ray Wilkins, 32 matches with my Forest colleague Peter Shilton and 29 alongside Kenny Sansom.

Just for the record I played with:

Terry Butcher 25 times, Bryan Robson and Phil Neal 24, Dave Watson 23, Steve Coppell and Kevin Keegan 20 and Mick Mills on 19 occasions.

I played with Tony Woodcock, a Nottingham Forest team-mate, in 13 games, the most memorable being when we both scored a brace against Northern Ireland in Belfast in October 1979, in a 5-1 victory in a European Championship qualifying game. We both scored in the friendly against Spain in the Nou Camp in Barcelona in March 1980. This was clearly a partnership we enjoyed; there was an immediate understanding between the two of us. Our greatest strength was our pace and, given time, we would have flourished as a partnership. But this never happened because he moved to Germany to join Cologne in November 1980 and we were never again selected together.

In 1993 I had a visit from Jimmy Armfield, representing the Football Association, to informally discuss the vacant England manager's job. I was happy at Sheffield Wednesday at the time and so things never progressed. Terry Venables was appointed the following year.

I have spoken about Bobby Robson but I feel it appropriate to mention both Don Revie and Ron Greenwood.

Obviously I am indebted to Don for giving me my debut and was privileged to work with him because, in my opinion, the Leeds United team of the early 70s was the best club team I played against; to be selected by someone who really knew his football made it all the more special.

However, he tried to create a club atmosphere within the England camp and I felt quite uncomfortable about the whole thing. The night before a game we would meet up to play carpet bowls, carpet putting and the dreaded bingo. Seriously, I couldn't wait for the sessions to finish. By nature I am a winner but I dreaded the thought of winning at bingo. Why? Because the prize was to call the numbers for the next game in the style of a professional bingo caller. Can you believe it? At the time I was a relatively shy person and the thought of having to shout 'house' filled me with dread.

A special thing about the Revie days was that before a Wembley fixture he would take the squad to Highbury (Arsenal's old ground) for a massage and a hot bath – nothing particularly special about that other than it was Don or our trainer Les Cocker that performed the massage!

There is little to say about Ron Greenwood, who was a lovely man. Tactically he was very aware and always wanted the game to be played right. A case in point was a match against Switzerland that we were losing 0-2. Ron decided to make a tactical switch at half-time, replacing me with Terry McDermott. I was disappointed, obviously, but Ron, who was always concerned about the feelings of his players, had come over to me and said, 'If you don't mind, I'm putting Terry McDermott on.' We were losing a World Cup match yet still this nice man didn't want to hurt my feelings!

My playing record by manager was:

Manager	Played	Won	Drew	Lost	For	Against
Don Revie	4	1	1	2	6	4
Ron Greenwood	28	16	6	6	48	19
Bobby Robson	20	8	7	5	23	12
Total	52	25	14	13	77	35

For each of my club teams I was able to bring international recognition: Birmingham City, 12 caps; Forest, 10; Manchester City, 10; Sampdoria, 20.

I always enjoyed playing for England against Scotland. During my career I played six times against the Tartan Army; it was always eventful.

My first game against the Scots was in June 1977 and my final tussle was in April 1986. Nine years of wonderful experiences at both Wembley and Hampden Park.

The game in 1977 lives long in many people's memories because the Scots won 2-1, their first victory at Wembley in ten years. Television cameras recorded the invasion of the pitch, which resulted in clumps of Wembley turf being transported across the border along with parts of the goals.

It was an incredible way to celebrate a long-awaited victory and the vision of those Scottish fans hanging from the crossbar until it broke is memorable.

I promised no statistics in my introduction to this book but I would like to record that against Scotland I was involved in four victories and two defeats.

In my Scottish debut at Wembley I was taken aback by the incredible support for Scotland. There must have been 70,000 in the stadium, which had a maximum capacity of 100,000. I wondered to myself how did they manage to get so many tickets!

On the way to the stadium the Tartan Army were there in their masses, decked out in their traditional kilts. As the coach approached them, they threw beer at it and I even saw their supporters run towards the bus to head butt it.

I do not think for a minute that they had had a few drinks!

The Scots had so many outstanding players to select from. In wide areas they had Peter Lorimer, Jimmy 'Jinky' Johnstone, Eddie Gray, Willie Johnston and John Robertson.

In midfield there was an absolute glut of talent: Billy Bremner, Graeme Souness, Archie Gemmill, Don Masson, Bruce Rioch and Asa Hartford.

The depth of their midfield options was evidenced by the fact that John McGovern, who won two league titles and two European Cups with Forest, was never picked for the national side because of the competition for places.

My first trip to Hampden Park was on 20 May 1978. When I went on to the pitch before the game I was aware of the very partisan atmosphere being created by the Scots, helped in no small way by the small contingent of English fans. In terms of the mix between home and away fans it was nothing like the year before.

We won 1-0 and I was involved in the goal. A cross came over and I challenged their goalkeeper Alan Rough, which resulted in the ball dropping loose. Steve Coppell got to it first and drilled it home. The goal was greeted with an eerie silence which I thought was due to the referee disallowing it for a foul by me on Rough.

That was not the case and the goal was allowed. The eerie silence was simply a disappointed Hampden Park!

On 27 May 1982 the FA Cup Final replay between Tottenham Hotspur and Queens Park Rangers was scheduled to take place. The England squad was based in Troon prior to the England v Scotland match on the following Saturday and it was planned that the squad would watch the replay on television.

In the squad there were a few avid music followers, including me, and we were aware that the Rolling Stones were performing at the Glasgow Odeon on that Thursday night.

Viv Anderson, Tony Woodcock, two others and I approached the manager Ron Greenwood to see if we could be excused from watching the replay so that we could go and see the Stones perform.

Ron was a really decent man and more than willing to agree to our request, and asked someone to ring through to the theatre to inform them that a number of the England squad were coming to the show.

Apparently the Stones were as excited as we were and their management invited us backstage. We went to their dressing room directly behind the stage. The room had a television and whilst chatting we found out that the Stones were as interested as we were in the outcome of the FA Cup Final replay.

The game went to extra time and therefore did not finish until after 9.30pm, which meant the Stones were late going on stage simply because they would not budge until the game had finished.

Slow handclaps were coming from the auditorium as it was now nearly 10 o'clock.

The manager of the Stones was getting very agitated and was desperate to get them on stage, so we were escorted from the dressing room area into the auditorium to take our seats. At that moment I realised that Keith Richards was following me and I turned around and told him, 'You have to go that way' pointing to the stage!

We watched the show, which was incredible, but obviously we were going to be much later getting back to Troon than we expected.

Nothing was said, though, as Ron Greenwood trusted his players implicitly.

My final game against the Scots was in 1986. Graeme Souness and I had played for Sampdoria against Napoli on the Sunday before the international. The following day we drove to Milan to meet up with Mark Hateley and Butch Wilkins, who were also in Italy, playing for AC Milan at the time, to catch a flight to London Heathrow airport. We all got on well and we enjoyed each other's company.

Two days later at 7.45pm at Wembley all that changed.

The ball broke free in the midfield and Graeme tackled Butch at waist height and at the same time almost decapitated him. There was never any friendship shown in an England v Scotland match.

As the song says, 'What a difference a day makes?' – well, two days in this instance.

Note: My full England career and goals appear as the Appendix.

Chapter Eleven

Birmingham City FC

240 games as manager in all competitions

LONG before I took over as manager of Birmingham City many fans and people in the game felt that I was destined to get that job at some stage in my career. Obviously I was excited about the thought of returning to St Andrew's but it had to be the right time. I was first approached about taking the hot seat back in the days when Dave Mackay was manager. Blues wanted me to become player-manager. As you would expect the offer was tempting but I declined because I was still playing in the first division and it was never an option for me to drop down into the third division.

Karren Brady made the initial contact about replacing Barry Fry, which, from an outsider's perspective, made absolute sense. I knew the club inside out and I had gained quite a bit of managerial experience having been at QPR and at Sheffield Wednesday for more than five years.

One or two discussions followed about the detail behind the deal, but I knew it was too good an opportunity to turn down. I was just a little bit reticent about returning to a football club where I had become a hero in the eyes of the supporters. Would their expectations be too much? If you were a betting man the odds would be stacked against anyone returning to their original football club and attempting to do what I had been tasked to do by the owners, and that was to get the club into the Premier League.

I didn't want to undo nine years of hero worship with the fans, and, although I was concerned about that, I had to back myself. I had plenty of confidence in my own ability and it has to be said that trying to getting promotion became an obsession with me. It took over, it became my life, it came before everything.

The reason for the managerial change at the club was obvious. The team was not doing well and was close to the bottom of the division when Barry Fry was dismissed.

My appointment was a wonderful opportunity for David Sullivan to make a statement about his commitment to the club as well as rekindle the enthusiasm of the fans who were on a low after a poor season. Sullivan knew that bringing me in would give the fans an enormous lift and set the club off in a new, positive direction.

When I took over as manager the youth system, where my career had started, no longer existed. I was keen to get a professional academy in place but that idea met with some opposition from David Sullivan. He wasn't keen on the time and expense that would be incurred in bringing young players through the system into the first team. He preferred to go talent spotting in the lower leagues. His idea was to give me £100,000. I would then instruct my chief scout to go out into the market to see who was available for a fee of £10,000. It meant we could buy up to ten players at £10,000 each and then see if they progressed enough at Blues for the club to make some money by selling them on at a profit. He was sure that there were suitable players in non-league football who our scouting network could find.

As you would expect from a businessman like David this made commercial sense but was not the way to get a club into the Premier League or even stay in Division One. And although that was his preference I managed to talk him out of the idea.

Dissuading him did not prove easy as he was convinced the idea had merit, but as a manager you are at your strongest when you first join a club. This being the case I was determined to get a youth system up and running, as I thought that it was important for the long-term development of the team and also because it ultimately gave the supporters what they loved to see – one of their own playing for the Blues!

Throughout my management stay at the club David loved a loan player. As far as he was concerned I could have as many loan players as I wanted. Why? Because they were not tied by a contract. So there it was, David Sullivan's recipe for success: a group of ex-non-league players augmented by a number of loan signings.

With regard to loan players, they can obviously benefit a team but it can also be a manager's selection burden, because, if you take a loan player from a top club, the club often demands that its loan players play regularly.

Apart from not having a youth system there were other areas where Birmingham was deficient.

The squad was far, far too big, which was hardly surprising given Barry Fry's transfer activities, and it had to be trimmed down. A lot of 'surgery' was needed which undoubtedly made that first season the toughest I have had in my management career.

My priorities became doing deals and trying to generate interest in players, which was time-consuming while all I really wanted to do was spend time on the training field rather than in the office on the telephone. So it was a particularly difficult first season but eventually the squad started to take shape.

The environment in which I was working was so inadequate. Some days at St Andrew's it would not be possible to go into my office because the rain would be coming through the ceiling – it was that bad.

Away from St Andrew's it was just as bad. At the start of that first season our training area was at the side of Damson Lane near Birmingham airport. This was close to where I used to train in the 70s. Quite nostalgic but that was all. The actual pitch we were training on was marked out incorrectly because it was the wrong size. Often training was delayed because Canadian geese were all over the pitch and their 'mess' needed cleaning up. The changing facilities were in a marquee!

Later we found the current training facility at Wast Hills, which we initially rented from the University of Birmingham. As soon as we took over we brought in Portakabins, which was a huge improvement for me. Previously I'd had to work from my office at St Andrew's or from the boot of my car. I was now given the luxury of a Portakabin!

So with Portakabins in place it was time to bring in my backroom staff. I was left to make my own choices which I appreciated and was delighted to appoint Mick Mills and Frank Barlow as assistant managers and Arvel Lowe as fitness coach. On the Academy side, initially I recruited Brian Eastick and then later got ex-Blues legend Bob Latchford to join me in developing the youngsters. Bob was good with the kids in the Academy sides. I think an ex-professional footballer in an Academy system is a must.

Although David Sullivan was keen on lower-league and loan players he was also generous enough to give me £2m to spend.

I was delighted, but there was a condition. He insisted that I had to make a big-name signing on a free transfer, to generate greater interest in the new season and kick-start season ticket sales. Not an easy task.

So my first signing had to be carefully considered. Who was out there? Who was a big name interested in coming to St Andrew's? I was aware that it was getting harder and harder to get that type of player on a free transfer but after much hard work I managed to pull off a major transfer coup by bringing in Steve Bruce. It came at a cost as he became, at the time, the highest paid footballer in the history of Birmingham City Football Club.

As I have said before fate is never far away in this type of situation, and this was the case in my appointment of Steve. In 1996 I was working as a commentator at the FA Cup Final between Manchester United and Liverpool. Steve had been left out of the United team and I had just got the Birmingham City manager's job.

I knew Steve would not be best pleased by Ferguson's decision to leave him out but I also knew he had a year left on his contract at Manchester United. I got on to Alex Ferguson about buying Steve.

What the deal amounted to was that we had to compensate Steve for his final year at Old Trafford, a year in which he could have had a testimonial. This made it an attractive and lucrative deal for Steve.

It was also a deal that laid down a marker – it showed that Birmingham City meant business as we had signed the Manchester United captain. It was a good move for him and he enjoyed his time playing at Birmingham.

It is not often that you get the chance to sign the captain of a team that has just won the double!

What I find pleasing is the fact that I signed both Gary Rowett and Steve Bruce who were both excellent players and probably, in the eyes of the Bluenoses, two of the best defenders in recent times. To see them develop their management careers since then, to the extent that they have both had successful periods managing Birmingham City, gives me enormous satisfaction.

The excellent business we did in the transfer market regarding Gary also gave the club enormous satisfaction. I bought him from Derby County in August 1998 for £1m and within two years we received £3m for him when he moved to Leicester City.

Not all transfers generate such handsome profits as that I achieved with Gary Rowett. I recall a young full-back who I'd signed from non-league Welling United for £100,000 called Steve Finnan. He played a handful of games before he went to Notts County for £300,000. At the time I considered that to be a decent profit but then he got converted to a winger and Kevin Keegan paid £600,000 to take him to Fulham. In the summer of 2003 he was transferred to Liverpool for £3.5m. Oh well, you can't win them all.

* * *

The mistake I made was not that I spent the money too quickly but that I assumed top players would accept the poor training facilities. The club didn't resemble a Championship club trying to get into the Premier League. The facilities were pretty abysmal and I had been quite shocked myself because I knew some non-league clubs had better facilities than Blues. That was where the mistake was: I brought in players from top-class Premier League teams who were probably even more shocked than I was when they came to Birmingham City.

They included Gary Ablett and Barry Horne from Everton, Paul Furlong from Chelsea and Mike Newell from Blackburn Rovers – I made a big mistake with all of them. It was a culture shock for these players who had played most of their football at top clubs.

I signed five players initially. Mike Newell was one of them and was a huge disappointment, as he came highly recommended by Alan Shearer who he had played with at Blackburn. Mike never really produced at Birmingham.

How it ended between Gary Ablett and the club was a matter of great sadness to me. Over a period of time we, meaning David Sullivan, Karren Brady and I, were negotiating a contract extension with Gary and his agent.

Nothing had been agreed and the deal had become protracted.

It was the Friday preceding our match against Crystal Palace on 9 February 1999 and, whilst we were doing our final preparations, Gary, aged 33 at the time, gave me the good news that he was happy to extend his contract and that I was to get the paperwork prepared for the following Monday when he would formally sign.

But 23 minutes into a 1-1 draw at Selhurst Park Gary ruptured his cruciate and medial knee ligaments and was destined to be out of the game for months and months. David Sullivan decided to withdraw the contract extension and after much uproar we said we would keep him on week-to-week terms after his deal expired in the June in order to assess his recovery and fitness.

Gary was out of action for eight and a half months and after a loan spell with Wycombe Wanderers in December 1999 he was told he would not be kept on at St Andrew's.

This was a horrible moment for me as Gary was one of my first signings and one of the nicest guys I have met in football.

He got the backing of the PFA so we ended up in a London tribunal in June 2000 at which Gary failed in his compensation claim over the contract. The tribunal felt that a verbal agreement was not binding.

This situation was extremely difficult for me because as much as I liked Gary I had to be loyal to my paymasters, which is a policy I have adopted throughout my career.

It was very sad when he died prematurely on New Year's Day 2012, after fighting non-Hodgkin's lymphoma, a form of blood cancer, for 16 months.

* * *

As I was trying to reshape the squad and also bring in new players I soon found myself having to make one or two big decisions. One was to sell Paul Peschisolido, Karren Brady's husband, to West Bromwich Albion in July 1996. It was normal procedure that I ring Karren, as managing director, to inform her of any transfer decisions. I told

Karren that I had accepted a fee of £600,000 from Albion for Paul and the telephone conversation went as follows:

KB: 'I like Paul living at home with me.'

TF: 'Well, he will still be able to. He's only going to West Bromwich. It's not a problem.'

Karren started to tell me what a good player Paul was and that he scored goals, to which I replied, 'I hear what you're saying but I've brought in Newell, I've brought in Furlong so I've got other forwards. The money I can generate from the sale of players will go to bringing in other players. This is my decision.'

KB: 'I was instrumental in bringing you into this club. If I'd known you were going to sell Paul I would never have done it.'

She used crude abusive language which shocked me. I was taken aback to say the least!

Karren made the point to me that Paul had signing-on fees due to which I said:

TF: 'Karren, as far as I'm concerned I've agreed a transfer fee that I think is a good deal for Birmingham City FC. However you want to deal with this now, whoever you want to talk to [i.e. Gold or Sullivan] then that's your prerogative but as far as I'm concerned I've made a footballing decision in the best interests of Birmingham City FC. Anything else now has nothing to do with me.'

Paul was a nice lad and a decent goalscorer. Accepting £600,000 was a good deal for the club, but this wasn't solely about money.

The biggest factor was what was happening in the dressing room.

One of the things I had learnt in my career was that you have to have a happy, harmonious dressing room.

With the greatest respect to Paul, I could sense that when he walked into the dressing room the other players would stop talking. Having the managing director's husband in the squad was not good for team spirit and it was no good for the lad. One or two of the senior players had come to me and said, 'Listen Boss, this is a bit of a problem with Paul, not so much Paul but his wife.' So agreeing to sell Paul was done first and foremost for the football club but also for the player.

Karren would have talked to Gold and Sullivan and what was said I don't know, but the deal went through regardless of the incredible hold Karren had over the two of them.

Whilst there were frustrations on the field there were moments of frustration for me regarding the way the owners did things from a commercial point of view.

Throughout my time at the club they never gave me a budget at the start of a season. This was something I always asked for but they never gave me one.

I'm the type of manager who, regardless of what the budget is, of how small or big it is, I can work to it as long as I know what it is and the lack of a budget made things difficult. Here is an example of why not having a budget that I could operate within made my life difficult.

Because I had no budget I had to ring David Sullivan every time I wanted to sign a player.

Once I got used to the need to go through this process I would usually have two or three options of players that I was interested in signing. The telephone calls always followed a pattern. Sullivan would ask me the player's name and I would tell him the first name on my list. He would then refer to the Rothmans Football Year Book. It's true, I am not joking.

He would look at the player, his age, his number of appearances and, if he was a forward, how many goals he had scored. No great conversation would take place and he would either agree or more likely say, 'No, who's the next one?'

That's how it was. I could give him a list of two or three players and if he didn't like them that was it – it was an incredibly difficult situation.

The way I liked to work was to watch players I thought could strengthen the team in certain areas. I would have a list of players for that position which I'd share with Mick Mills and Bernard Paintin, our chief scout.

If we were really serious about a player we would watch them playing at home and away. Before making a decision it was always preferable to watch them playing both home and away.

I would always have to go and watch players. I couldn't buy a player based on watching a video, which I know some managers do. I had to see them in the flesh and if possible talk to their previous coaches and managers to get an insight into what they were about in terms of whether they were good trainers, did they have good characters and whether they were trustworthy. It wasn't just about their ability to kick a football around; I had to go into a lot of things.

A lot of the players I brought in were good, honest, consistent players and they rarely let me down because I'd done my homework. There were times, because of an injury crisis, when we needed to get someone in quickly, when I thought the owners could have been a little more understanding.

The one thing I will not do – after all, they gave me five and a half years managing the club I love – is over-criticise the way they went about being owners of a football club.

In many ways it was different to what I had experienced previously, but it was their way and they were my bosses and therefore I respected them. I got enough opportunities with the tools I was given to win promotion. So there are no recriminations as far as I am concerned. I am not going to criticise them.

All I will say is that they could have done things slightly differently which would have simplified things and made things clearer for me, for example by giving me a budget. Let me explain.

I had given the owners a couple of striker options which they turned down. A couple of weeks later I had a call from David Sullivan who said, 'Can you get yourself down to St Andrew's?'

I asked why and he informed me that Barry Silkman was there.

Barry Silkman was a football agent and an ex-player, and was David's confidant. David leaned on him.

Once I turned up at the training ground to find a Brazilian player there. Nobody had even spoken to me about him and apparently he was having a trial. I knew nothing about it as David Sullivan had organised it with Barry Silkman.

Anyway, I got myself to the ground because I'd been told that Barry was there and 'his' player was having a medical. I was amazed that this could be happening without my knowledge. I rang David.

TF: 'Who is the player having a medical?'

DS: 'Dele Adebola, do you know him?'

TF: 'Yes, I know Dele but I haven't studied him. All I know is he's at Crewe and he's a big guy but I haven't watched him play. What's the fee?'

DS: 'About a million.'

TF: 'So what are you saying, take Dele or can I get someone else?'

DS: 'No, Dele or nothing.'

TF: 'OK, I'll do it.'

Later I got a call from David Sullivan:

DS: 'Dele's passed his medical and as Karren is away, can you get the cheque book from her office. It's in the right-hand drawer of her desk and write out a cheque for Barry Silkman for £84,000.'

Obviously I signed the cheque on behalf of the club and got it to Barry.

Things were always done differently. I used to speak with David Sullivan practically every day, as I did with Karren. David Gold was never working on a day-by-day basis at the club which was why I thought it was imperative to have board meetings on a regular basis, because often on a matchday David Gold would want to see me, talk about football and find out what was happening. He wasn't always kept totally informed, so it made it quite difficult for him because he didn't know all of what was going on. We had one board meeting before a night game at about 6 o'clock. It only lasted for half an hour because David Sullivan was more concerned with how many spectators were coming through the turnstiles.

The following day Karren asked me how the meeting had gone and my response was that it had been a bit of a waste of time as it had lasted no more than half an hour. I told her I thought formal board meetings were absolutely vital.

I understood why it was difficult – David Gold and David Sullivan lived in Essex and they could not be bothered to come up to Birmingham for meetings. I stressed the point that I thought these meetings were of great importance. Karren said that she would try and get one arranged for when we were next playing in London.

She looked at the fixtures and saw that we were at Queens Park Rangers on a Saturday in three weeks' time. She suggested the Friday night for our board meeting as we would have travelled down the night before in preparation for the game.

I reluctantly agreed because it was not the right time to have a meeting. The night before games my mind was quite rightly on how we would try and win three points the following day.

Karren promised to come back with the time and venue. When she did I was absolutely astonished – the meeting was scheduled for 9.30pm at Stringfellows Night Club in Soho.

At that moment I started laughing, saying that the suggestion was ridiculous. But more importantly what went through my mind was, 'This is my football club and has been for many, many years.' I get stressed-out at times and on many occasions I have put the football club ahead of my family. I have actually shed tears for Birmingham City Football Club and the idea of going to Stringfellows really shocked me. For me, it put everything into perspective in terms of how they saw things compared to me. Can you imagine us trying to conduct a board meeting there? What would the fans think of their club owners in a nightclub, discussing club-related private matters?

Here is an example of the way I feel about money and the way things were. At this time, Birmingham City was going for membership of the Alternative Investment

Market. I had to devote two or three days during this particular week to going to London to meet business people.

I had to read up on what needed to be said. I did what I had to do because I was helping Birmingham City. A lot of what I was asked to say wasn't 100 per cent accurate and I resented the time I missed at the training ground and with the players. David Sullivan, Karren Brady, me and the lawyer Henri Brandman were involved.

Towards the end of the week Henri made some comment to me to which I replied, 'To be honest, I'm doing all this for the football club. I am not getting a penny for it. I'm a football coach, I want to be on the training pitch. I do not want to be in two or three meetings a day in London. I don't get even a "thank you" for it.' That was that as far as I was concerned.

Anyway, the following day Karren said, 'I hear you've been having a bit of a moan to Henri.' I said, 'Not so much a moan but I would like, every now and then, a little recognition, a little bit of a thank you for what I am doing, because this is not what I'm at the club for.'

Karren came back to me later saying that David Sullivan had told her to give me a cheque for £10,000. I said, 'It's very nice and, possibly, if this had been thought of by yourselves I would willingly have accepted it, but that's not the case.'

I got the cheque and tore it up and put it in the bin, saying, 'It's not about how much it is or what it is, it could have been as simple as a bouquet of flowers for my wife. What it should be about is showing that you are pleased with what I am doing and showing gratitude.'

That mention of my wife Helen reminds me of a couple of things. She was totally supportive of every move I made. In our first year at Blues Helen and I lived temporarily in a friend's flat on the Bristol Road. Helen was my biggest ... I was going to say 'fan I had' but she, along with the boys, went to every game home and away and she played a big part in my management style.

I had learnt from Brian Clough how to look after players' wives. He would often give them little presents because his philosophy, which became mine, was 'keep the wives happy and the players will be happy'.

Helen would often arrange little evening events, maybe take over a restaurant, at which players and their wives would be present. We'd have a nice dinner together and I would always be there with them. Maybe I'd invite Jasper Carrott along with his guitar and he'd do a few songs, things like that.

Helen played a big part as she also looked after the wives down at the ground. She took it upon herself to do that and played a huge part in my management at Birmingham City – unpaid, naturally. On one occasion, however, her hospitality backfired.

When Helen and I were living in Wentworth she invited David Gold's mother and David Sullivan's mother to join her and her mother for afternoon tea at our home.

During tea, David Gold's mother asked, 'You know what my son does, what his living is?' She explained that he was in the world of pornography – not the normal topic of conversation at high tea. 'At the moment he's making a talking vibrator for the executive businessman,' she added. Helen's mother almost choked on her piece of cake!

David Sullivan would often, on a Friday afternoon, contact me to get my feelings about the following day's game. He would tell me the bookies' odds for our games, particularly when we were due to face teams in the lower echelons of the league.

It was his way of using our position as red-hot favourites to bring about a win. He wanted me to tell the players there was no room for complacency.

This was a good use of betting odds but I felt it was used in bad taste on another occasion, when I knew his elderly mother had suffered a bad fall in the bath. I rang David to enquire how his mother was and he replied that she had had a bad fall and was in the bath for some time before she was found. He thought she had a 1/2 odds on chance of survival.

The use of betting odds to inform me of his mother's prognosis was in my opinion a little odd and very unexpected.

I am proud of what I achieved in what some might call difficult circumstances although naturally I was disappointed not to get to the Premier League or win the Worthington Cup.

It takes some effort to get to the play-offs on three consecutive occasions. We played Watford in 1999, Barnsley in 2000 and Preston North End in 2001.

We should have beaten Watford in the first one, the Preston game was a huge disappointment, terrible, and the Barnsley play-off was a freak result. Barnsley's manager was Dave Bassett who was a pal of mine from our days in Sheffield when I was managing the Owls and he was looking after the Blades. I know, because he told me, that they came to St Andrew's that afternoon looking for a 0-0 draw, yet they went away with a 0-4 win – just an absolute freak result, probably the worst result of my managerial career. The next few days leading up to the second leg were the toughest I have experienced because, with the best will in the world, when you are 4-0 down … The following year we went to Preston and once again things went against us in the game. When we lost I wondered if the owners would make a change.

Why is it that the Football League and UEFA have different rules on away goals? If the game at Preston had been a UEFA Champions League or Europa League semi-final we would have gone through to the final.

A couple of years after I left Birmingham as manager the FA Vase Final was played at St Andrew's and I was asked to be guest of honour and to meet the players. I sat and had lunch with Geoffrey Thompson, chairman of the Football Association, and on the television in the background a play-off game was on. I mentioned to Geoffrey this difference between the away goals rule. His response was, 'I did not

Graeme Souness, Ray Wilkins (AC Milan) and me

Sampdoria v Napoli – trying to get away from Maradona

With Mancini and Vialli

Helen and me on an Italian rainy day

Johan Cruyff, who asked for my England debut shirt

Home or away – proud to wear the England shirt

Pele – my hair stylist

Scoring against Denmark – Bobby Robson's first match on 22 September 1982

England 1982 team group

Opening game of 1982 World Cup v France on 16 June 1982

Czechoslovakia goal celebration on 20 June 1982

1982 World Cup action

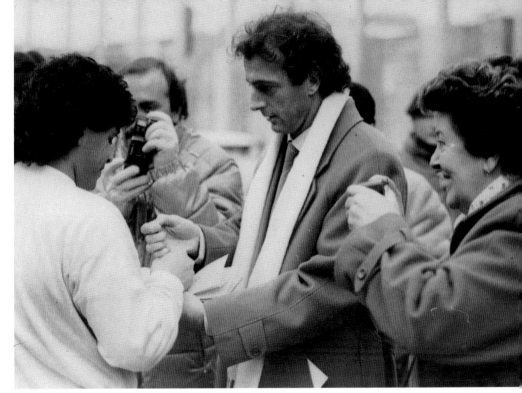

My mom Phyl taking my photograph with Maradona in Italy

One season with Glasgow Rangers

QPR – player/manager

Celebrating with Mark Bright and David Hirst at Sheffield Wednesday

Crystal Palace – manager

know that.' I confirmed that the UEFA rule did not apply in the Football League but did in Europe, to which he replied, 'We have a meeting next week. I am going to make a point to bring that up at our FA meeting.' But as we now know it was all words and nothing got changed.

In the lead-up to the Worthington League Cup Final one or two of the games were amazing. In the semi-final first leg we had lost 0-1 to Ipswich but in the second leg the atmosphere was unbelievable, it was just fantastic. The pitch was deteriorating and that night I changed tactics. I would not allow anything to be played short from the back into midfield, everything had to go long simply because of the pitch. George Burley, the Ipswich manager, had an excellent footballing team and they attempted to play the kind of football that they were capable of, which was very stylish. But they found it incredibly difficult on a pitch which resembled a vegetable patch. We won the match comfortably 4-1, it was a brilliant night and we were in the final.

I said to David Sullivan, 'We've still got a chance of promotion and as far as I'm concerned I'm still looking at automatic promotion but the only chance we've got of doing it is if you re-lay this pitch.' He said, 'It would cost £100,000 and I am not prepared to do it. You won on that pitch, you carry on winning.' The next match we played at home to Wolves and they beat us 1-0 and harsh words were exchanged between David Sullivan and myself!

In the Worthington Cup Final against Liverpool I felt a little bit let down because we went to the Millennium Stadium and gave a fantastic account of ourselves. Once again we did not have much luck. Nobody can tell me that ref David Elleray did not get it wrong with the challenge of Henchoz on Johnson. It was a definite penalty. One of the things that made me so proud to be Birmingham manager was the way we took Liverpool all the way to a penalty shoot-out. During my time we rarely underperformed. You could question a lot of things about individual players and the way that we played but in terms of effort my teams were second to none. We even scored seven goals twice in 1998, beating Stoke 7-0 in the January and Oxford 7-1 in the December.

Team selection has never been a problem for me. I hear that certain managers have to deliberate long and hard on who will play where. How difficult it is to pick someone ahead of someone else when you know your players so well? To drop Jerry Gill and David Burrows from the starting 11 for the final was a decision taken purely on footballing reasons. Jerry, who I liked very much, took my decision well but Burrows had the opposite attitude and made his feelings known to me on the pitch. It was a big day for everyone and his only concern was for himself, which unfortunately is fairly typical of most footballers. He showed a lack of respect to me and everyone else associated with the club.

After the Worthington Cup Final it was pointed out to me that the referee consulted the Chief of Police for Cardiff about which end the penalties should be taken from should the game require them and it was no surprise that he advised the Liverpool end, because he was a Liverpool fan!

I remembered this when we got to Preston for the semi-final of the play-offs. I made a point of going on to the pitch when the referee, Paul Danson, and his linesman were there. In front of the linesmen I said: 'At Cardiff we had to take penalties at the Liverpool end so if this game happens to go to penalties you've got a building site at one end and the other end is full of Preston supporters, which would be a huge advantage for them if you decide to take the penalties to that end. I assume it's going to be the other end where the building site is.' He acknowledged that. Sod's law prevailed of course and it went to penalties, and I got absolutely hammered because I was seen in front of the television cameras taking my team off the pitch. What I was trying to do was to get them into the tunnel area so I could talk to the referee out of the view of the cameras. Anyway, the referee would not have it. I don't know what happened after that moment on the pitch at 6.30pm but I wouldn't mind guessing that Sky Sports, which was covering the game, had a huge influence over which end the penalties were taken, because, being a media man myself, I know you do not want to see the penalties kicked into an end that is derelict.

I got hammered, and to this day people still go on about it being one of those big talking points. I get accused of not wanting to take the penalties but that was never the case. I wanted to win the game fairly through taking penalties. I got hauled up by the Football Association and the referee denied there was any conversation prior to the match. He claimed that it was always going to be at that end and I was given a heavy fine of £1,500.

In my second season, in the very last game of the season, we had a chance to get into the play-offs. We were playing Charlton Athletic and their goalkeeper played fantastically and denied us that chance. I thought it would be a good idea to reward the players with a trip away for a few days, which is quite normal within the game when you are successful.

I felt that it would be good to say a bit of a thank you to the players, who had worked really hard to get us close to the play-offs, and it would set us up nicely for the start of the new season. I priced up a little trip to Marbella, staying in a four-star hotel, which came to between £7,000 and £8,000 in all. It was met with a refusal from Karren Brady, who had referred it to David Sullivan. I put my case that this trip was important for team bonding and that it would set us up nicely to give it a go the next season. Regardless of what I said it was still a 'No.' I told David Sullivan and Karren Brady that I would be prepared to pay for the trip out of my own money, as I felt quite strongly about the matter.

Although I was not thrilled about spending between £7,000 and £8,000 of my own money, I thought it would benefit the club and it would benefit me in the long run.

So I was prepared to pay for the trip and then to my surprise I got a call from David Gold saying that he had heard about what I had proposed and that he and his brother Ralph would like to help. I expressed my gratitude and appreciation and then they announced that they were prepared to give a £1,000 each towards the trip.

I smile about it because when I heard David Gold on the telephone telling me he wanted to help I really thought he was going to say that he would pay for all of it, not just make a donation. It was typical that his offer came after I had said I would pay, so I said, 'Thank you very much, David, it's a nice gesture but I prefer to pay for it myself.'

Within 24 hours Karren, who had been speaking to David Sullivan, called to say that they had agreed to pay for the trip. It was the right result in the end but it was wearing me down having to deal with this type of issue. I am a football man and all I wanted to do was go on the training field, work with the players and try to produce results on matchdays. That's what I wanted to do – all these other things were distractions.

Another instance was when I signed Peter Ndlovu from Coventry City. His transfer fee had to be renegotiated due to a problem highlighted by the scan in his medical. After an initial payment to Coventry it was agreed that we would pay additional money based on when he made an appearance for the first team.

Peter was a clever player, a match-winner on his day, but he blew hot and cold and could be very inconsistent. He could make things happen and there was a period when I used him from the bench for either 15 or 20 minutes depending on the situation. After two or three appearances by Peter from the bench, I received a fax from David Sullivan asking me, because of the money being paid to Coventry every time he played, not to play him spasmodically for short periods of time as the club was having to pay the full appearance amount each time. I was being asked to make decisions related to football on a financial basis and I agreed to do it with a great deal of reluctance. In reality I played Peter when I felt he could help the team to get a good result.

Similar interference happened with Christian Poulsen, who is mentioned in my introduction, a 21-year-old defensive midfielder playing for FC Copenhagen who I was interested in bringing to St Andrew's in 2001.

It was normal transfer policy for me to negotiate the transfer fee with the selling club and salaries, bonuses, etc., with the player. Obviously I was given guidelines by both Karren and David Sullivan as to what sort of figures should be offered, which was acceptable to me.

On this occasion the fee had been agreed between the two clubs and I was given permission to speak to the player. This being the case it was agreed that Christian and his parents would come over to England and meet me at St Andrew's, with a view to him signing a contract.

On my way to the meeting I received a telephone call from Karren, which was unusual, telling me not to say anything to the player regarding salary, etc. When I arrived at the ground Christian and his parents were there along with Karren.

Without discussing matters with me, she offered him a deal which I considered to be a poor offer. It was an offer that he was sure to refuse. I could see the disappointment on his face, because all he wanted to do was agree a financial package and sign a contract for the Blues. An opportunity was missed because he was young and talented. I would not have thought that Karren would have followed the progress of young Christian Poulsen but I did follow his career with interest.

After winning the Danish Superliga championship with FC Copenhagen he moved to Germany. He joined FC Schalke 04 for €7m before moving to Spain where he won the UEFA Cup with Sevilla. His tour of Europe continued, with spells in Italy and England, playing for Juventus and Liverpool respectively. He returned to FC Copenhagen in 2014 after going to France with Evian and Holland with Ajax.

When I first saw him in 2001 he was an established member of the Denmark Under-21 side and in the same year won his first full international recognition. He eventually gained 92 caps for his country, scoring six goals and featuring in the 2002 World Cup, the 2004 European Championship and the 2010 World Cup.

He was named Danish Player of the Year in 2005 and 2006 and was the first player to win the award in consecutive years.

After doing all my research into the player, I felt certain he would be a success, which was proved by the quality of the clubs he played for. I just wish Birmingham City could have been on that list as he, as I predicted, developed into a very good footballer.

The 2001/02 season started and things were not going great, but we started to pick up results and then went away to Man City in the League Cup and I played a lot of reserves to save players for the league games. We were heavily beaten 0-6.

I am pretty sure that the decision to dismiss me was made that night, because on the Friday we went up to Barnsley and I was sitting in the lounge when I had a phone call from someone whose voice I thought I recognised but I couldn't be certain. The mystery person said, 'You're fucking sacked this weekend' and put the phone down! We played the match against Barnsley and we beat them convincingly and throughout the game the fans never stopped singing my name, from the first to the 90th minute. Who knows, perhaps they sensed something was happening.

On the following Monday I was called to St Andrew's where I was met by Karren and David Gold, who said that they were going to make a change as a lot of things had happened recently with which they weren't happy.

There was an agreement in my contract stating that if I left the football club my new club would have to pay Birmingham City compensation, and if the club was getting rid of me they were required to pay a year's salary, which was £200,000.

They came up with a reason why they weren't going to pay me the £200,000. It was not the money but I was so hurt by this attitude because I had given everything to the football club and in the end, when it happened, I have to admit it was a bit of a relief.

I would have accepted their decision graciously, because it had reached a point when it was right for it to happen. Two or three weeks before I had said to them, 'Listen, if I could make it easy for you now, if you really want me to go, let's sort it now by paying up my contract and I will go. We can shake hands. We've had a great five and a half years. I've given it my best and we go out as friends.' They replied, 'No, no, we want you to stay on.'

Anyway, two to three weeks later they decided that it had to happen but they did not want to pay the £200,000. I looked at them, then I looked at David Gold, and said, 'OK, then as far as I'm concerned let's end the meeting. I'll give this to my lawyers and they can deal with it.' 'No, No.' said David Gold. 'Give me five minutes.' They didn't need five minutes, they went away and within two minutes came back with a cheque for the full amount and gave it to me. I looked at the date on the cheque – it was the previous

Friday! It had obviously been written before the Barnsley match. I felt they had acted like absolute shits – all I could think of was how I had given everything to *my* club!

I could give you a hundred stories but I am not going to write a book on my time as manager of Birmingham City Football Club, because these people are not important enough for me to devote a whole book to them.

I think I've been more than fair to them. I didn't have to say they gave me every opportunity. I have no need for recriminations and I am not going to criticise them, but they could have made it easier for me. The money they used to give me was kind of drip fed.

We had five and a half years together and that's a long time in football. We had some nice times with my wife and we'd go out with David Sullivan – not often, but Helen used to sit with them at every away game and we got to know each other fantastically well. I think it's rather sad that, as grown-up men and women, when a business relationship comes to an end, we can't remain friends. That's always been my feeling. If I do a job of work for people who are paying me and eventually they no longer want my services it doesn't mean that we start criticising each other and stop being friends.

The agreement was that I walked away with a cheque and I would not bad-mouth anybody at the club, which I have adhered to for 17 years. The agreement was binding on all parties. However, within a week of my sacking David Sullivan was slagging me off in a huge double-page spread in the *Sunday Mercury*. David Gold wrote a book in 2006 and devoted a whole chapter to me, entitled 'Golden Boy'. The title was probably the only complimentary thing he said.

When you are working together in a football club, and you have day-to-day contact with David Sullivan and Karren Brady, of course there's going to be certain things that happen, but in the end I am a great believer in shaking hands and remaining friends no matter what happened during that time.

There was no contact after Helen's death, no call, no e-mail, which says a lot about them. She was acknowledged as being extremely popular. She was a loving and caring person and it's absolutely disgusting that they couldn't find the time to send a card or pick up the phone, particularly after all she had done for the football club.

Helen's funeral was like a who's who of football. It was just extraordinary. Graeme Souness took me to one side at the wake and put his arms around me. He couldn't talk because he was crying but eventually he said, 'Let me tell you, every man in there would have liked to have had Helen as their wife.'

Shortly after I left the club I became Crystal Palace manager and within six weeks I had to bring my team to St Andrew's. Some of the staff were looking forward to seeing us but in the week before the game someone from the board told the staff not to give Helen Francis access to anywhere near the tunnel area. How disappointing is that?

When I left, Steve Bruce and I did something of a swap deal, as he came to Birmingham City as I went to Crystal Palace. For a while, when we saw each other, things didn't feel the same. I felt there was something Steve wanted to talk to me about. Was it because he didn't feel comfortable about taking my job?

One day we got to talk it through and he said to me, 'I felt bad taking your job.' I said, 'Steve, let me tell you, I was absolutely thrilled that one of my players got the Birmingham job,' and it was like a weight off his shoulders. He could not believe what he was hearing; I was so pleased that he was appointed. I always remember Karren Brady saying to Steve that whenever Trevor Francis's time's up you'll always be welcome back here as manager.

I think that's wrong but not surprising – whenever we were on a losing streak the rumour was that Steve Bruce would take my job.

Reflecting on the play-offs, they created a strange situation because the season finished in May but not for us because we were in the play-offs. On the one hand the season had been successful but within ten days it could be deemed a failure. I was in three lots of play-offs, three semi-finals, but never got to a final. If you look at it, we had three semi-finals in six games of football, losing three and winning three but still never getting to a final!

I hate talking about things that went against me but Jasper Carrott often says, 'You had plenty of luck; unfortunately it was all bad!'

There was huge disappointment amongst the fans but I never felt any antipathy towards me because I was one of them so they knew it hurt me as much as it did them.

As I have said we never had formal board meetings but we used to have end-of-season chats at David Sullivan's house. I used to go with Mick Mills and we would talk about the season just gone and our hopes for the new campaign, what our thoughts were regarding new signings and what sort of money would be available. After three play-offs, the last little chat we had down in Essex went along the lines of: for the forthcoming season let's not bother about the play-offs – let's go for automatic promotion. That was the first time that this had been said. I was fine with it, even though it obviously meant that pressure was being applied.

I asked, 'What money is going to be available?' to which they replied, 'No money is available. If you want to strengthen the squad then you will have to generate the money yourself.'

I could not believe what I was hearing so I said to David Sullivan, 'David, would it be fair to say that I have got a greater desire than you to get Birmingham City into the Premier League?' He said, 'Yes, I think that's fair, but I think we should keep that between us.' I thought that was very revealing. I knew it was a make or break year for me! I sensed this would be my last season if we didn't get promotion.

When I was trying to trim down the playing squad I had inherited from Barry Fry I met up with Dave Webb who was manager of Brentford at the time and we talked about him possibly taking Ricky Otto.

We were discussing the footballing merits of Ricky and I happened to mention Ricky's background, which was difficult, to say the least. Without knowing the details I was aware that he had a huge scar across his abdomen which was the result of a fight.

I could see that Dave was interested in Ricky so I asked him whether he would take him. He paused, deliberated, gave himself lots of thinking time and then replied that he would prefer to take the guy who had given him his scar!

David Sullivan was a man who liked a gamble. He also liked to exploit his investment in Birmingham City Football Club. An example of this was when Rod Stewart, the rock legend, was selling his house, which was near to David's home in Essex. David wanted to buy the property for his partner Eve. As they were negotiating the price it became evident that there was a sum of £10,000 upon which neither of them was prepared to budge.

Knowing that Rod was keen on his football and not without talent, David suggested a penalty shoot-out for the disputed £10,000 in Rod Stewart's back garden where he had a football pitch.

He contacted me and explained the situation and asked whether I could get Paul Furlong to travel to David's home in Essex to take his penalty against Rod.

I had no problem with the suggestion and arranged for Paul to travel after a day's training.

In the end the shoot-out never happened and I still don't know whether David or Rod backed down over the £10,000 difference in their house price valuations.

Chapter Twelve
Crystal Palace FC

92 games as manager in all competitions

I WAS out of football for a short while after leaving Birmingham City and was getting itchy feet, knowing that I had at least one more high-profile job in me.

I still had great enthusiasm for the game and knew that, given the opportunity, I could add value to any club.

That opportunity came in the form of Simon Jordan, who was owner and chairman of Crystal Palace. I was attracted to Palace because joining them did not mean a drop down the leagues, I enjoyed working in London and it was going to be interesting, as it was almost like a 'swap' deal between Steve Bruce and me. Here I was, potentially going to Selhurst Park as Steve took over the managerial reins at St Andrew's.

In the middle of November I flew to Marbella, Spain for what turned out to be an interesting meeting.

Simon conducted the interview, speaking openly about himself and the club. He talked passionately about his plans for Crystal Palace. He was very forthright in his views; this was a guy with strong feelings and opinions.

When it was my time to speak I knew he was wanting a similar passionate response, as he knew all about what I had achieved at Birmingham City. I felt it was my job to lose. I mentioned something that he particularly liked and he responded well. My reaction surprised him and he freely admitted that this was the type of passion he wanted from his new manager.

I was offered the job on a salary of £320,000 per annum and agreed to work alongside the existing coaching staff.

My appointment prompted a mixed response from both Birmingham and Palace supporters. Blues fans were clearly disappointed about my leaving even though Steve Bruce was known to them. To say the Palace fans were not particularly excited about me going there was an understatement. So there we were, two new managerial appointments and both sets of fans disappointed.

The season started very well for Crystal Palace and it reinforced my feeling that I had made the right decision – Simon wanted me despite his initial misgivings, to the extent that he sold the club to me with impressive passion and promised me there was money to spend.

* * *

As often happens in life, fate again took a hand resulting in the ITV Digital deal collapsing due to low audience figures, piracy issues and an ultimately unaffordable multi-million-pound deal with the Football League. This had massive implications for the Football League as ITV Digital proposed to reduce its annual payments, paying only £50 million for its remaining two years of the Football League deal, a £129 million pay cut. Chiefs from the League said that any reduction in the payment could threaten the existence of many football clubs, who had budgeted for large incomes from the television contract.

* * *

This decision made life very difficult for everyone including Crystal Palace and the inevitable spending cuts were put in place through no fault of Simon Jordan. The major reduction in the club's purchasing power in the transfer market made my job increasingly difficult. I knew our good start to the season meant that we were punching well above our weight. As I had had five-plus years in the division with Birmingham City I was able to assess the squad with great accuracy. I knew the strengths and weaknesses of each member of the squad and could relate them to the players I had managed at Birmingham. I could not understand how Palace were riding so high in the league with the players we had; it was clearly unsustainable. To maintain our position in the league I needed to bring in better players but with a restriction on my transfer budget this was going to prove difficult.

I signed Kit Symons, Danny Granville and Ade Akinbiyi, with mixed results it would be fair to say. But my major success was getting Andrew Johnson to Selhurst Park.

Steve Bruce had always wanted Clinton Morrison and eventually he joined Steve for £5m but I insisted that as part of the deal we got Andrew Johnson (AJ) as a makeweight, valued at £400,000. Andy went on to become one of Crystal Palace's best strikers, eventually gaining international recognition for England.

I wanted to link him with Ade Akinbiyi, who I had bought from Leicester City for £2.25m and who was on a significant salary. It will be no surprise to anyone that I am a great lover of pace and players that want to work hard for their team.

Andrew and Ade were two guys who could attack from the front but also could be our best defenders!

I saw this as a partnership that would take us to greater heights.

Unfortunately, shortly after signing, Akinbiyi ruptured his cruciate knee ligaments resulting in him hardly ever playing for Palace, making only 11 starts in two seasons.

In fairness, even prior to the rupture, he had shown himself to be rather limited in his technical ability and he was not well received by the Selhurst Park faithful. In hindsight I should not have pushed Simon to give me the required transfer fee. I really pushed him, certain that Ade was the answer as a partner for Andrew. The situation did not increase my popularity with the Palace fans. All fans like to see their players show some level of technical ability and I soon realised that I had made a mistake with Akinbiyi. The situation I had created did little to enhance my relationship with Simon, either.

We had a relationship where he was very much the boss, he knew exactly what he wanted and, to be fair to him, he had a good understanding of the game.

Because of his appearances in the media and the manner in which he talked, he did little to endear himself to the general public. People thought he was flash and arrogant, but there was a side to him that I really liked. Simon was a contradiction in many ways. On occasions, when it was necessary, he could be very complimentary but if he felt it appropriate he could be incredibly rude and aggressive. He was particularly intimidating on the phone and for anyone with a nervous disposition or who was less experienced, unlike me, he could be frightening.

It's true to say that there were not many high spots during my time at Crystal Palace. One, though, was beating our local neighbours, Brighton and Hove Albion. I never quite understood why they were deemed local neighbours when they were at least 25 miles away. Nevertheless it was a keenly contested rivalry and we thoroughly enjoyed beating them 5-0 at Selhurst Park in October 2002, when AJ scored three, including a penalty! He also got a hat-trick at Walsall on the following Tuesday night in a match we won 3-4. Not bad – two hat-tricks in consecutive games. He was a very good player and one of my successes.

Another high point was when we knocked Liverpool out of the FA Cup at Anfield in 2003. With the highs there were the lows, though, and one particular low point involved my spat with our substitute goalkeeper.

It was the second game of the 2002/03 season at Selhurst Park. I was standing in the technical area when Bradford broke on the counter-attack and scored on 75 minutes.

Disappointed, I went back to the dugout and I happened to look at our Latvian reserve goalkeeper Aleksander Kolinko, who was laughing.

I walked over to him and said, 'What are you fucking laughing at?' He continued laughing. I was so upset at losing the goal and at his attitude that I hit him on the chin with my right fist. His head went back and hit the back of the dugout.

At that moment I realised what I had done. As often happens in these situations, by chance the fourth official happened to be looking over at the dugout as I did it and immediately signalled to the referee who stopped the game. After what seemed a short discussion between the two officials I was sent to the stand. The game was drawn at 1-1. We equalised four minutes after I was dismissed.

After the game, Simon came to ask me what had happened. After I had told him, I then spoke to the player quietly, away from the others, and tried to apologise. I said my action was 'totally out of character'.

Understandably at the time, he wouldn't have anything to do with my apology. His only comment was, 'This would not have happened back in my country.'

Then I spoke to the police as they had got involved, along with the media. The player referred the matter to his agent, who demanded £50,000 from Simon Jordan. Simon was told that if no payment was forthcoming his agent would take it further on behalf of his player.

In the meantime I was asked to go to Selhurst Park to see Simon. He could have sacked me because this was gross misconduct and undoubtedly a sackable offence. Simon was extremely good about the matter and limited my punishment to a written warning, which was serious because a second warning would have seen me dismissed.

He admitted that he quite admired my attitude, my desire and my will to win. Even though he felt this way, as the owner and chairman of the football club he had to do what was correct, even though deep down I do not believe he wanted to do it.

The media really got into the incident and it was reported as follows:

> The Crystal Palace goalkeeper, Alex Kolinko, will sit next to Trevor Francis on the bench this afternoon despite the bad blood between them. Kolinko claims he was hit in the face by his manager during Tuesday night's draw with Bradford City.

Francis was sent to the stands by the fourth official following the incident, but later tried to brush it aside, saying it was a reaction to Kolinko laughing when Bradford scored.

'I was not laughing in the dugout,' Kolinko said. 'The manager punched me on the nose. I have not been given an explanation why he did it. My nose is very sore and bruised.'

Neither the police nor Kolinko have pressed charges so far. The player's agent Phil Graham denied that the goalkeeper had made a complaint.

'Alex is surprised and disappointed that he has not received an official apology from the manager and is very upset that he is being portrayed as an uncaring professional,' Graham said. He did not report the incident to the police. An on-duty policeman next to the dugout saw what happened and the policeman told Alex he would be writing a report.

The Metropolitan Police admitted yesterday that the matter was not yet closed. 'We're still investigating an allegation of common assault,' a Scotland Yard spokesman said.

Francis had talks with Kolinko yesterday and the goalkeeper was included in Palace's reserve team in the game against Bournemouth on Wednesday.

Simon Jordan, the Palace chairman, is keen for the matter to be forgotten. 'I have spoken to both parties and Trevor has apologised to the player because it was an inappropriate reaction,' Jordan said. 'The player is entitled to his opinion but we have two alleged incidents here and I wasn't there to see either of them. We have an alleged incident where a player was seen to be smirking after a goal and an alleged incident of him being clipped around the ear. Both are unfortunate and inappropriate. The player has played for the club for four years and there is no history of problems between the player and the manager. This is an internal club matter and it is closed. I have acted appropriately. I would like to think we can go forward and resolve this situation in an amicable fashion.'

Kolinko's position at the club is now in doubt. He is no longer considered the No.1, with Matt Clarke the preferred choice in goal.'

Simon's brother Dominic was very hands-on at the football club, as was his father, who was the most avid watcher of every Crystal Palace team.

When money became a little tight at the club and we were no longer in with a shout of getting into the play-offs we had a fundamental disagreement: I wanted to finish as high as possible but Simon said he wasn't prepared to pay for mediocrity. He insisted that some of the regular first team starters be dropped, forcing me to play some of the younger reserve team players.

Simon was very much influenced by his father. I remember a young defender Will Antwi, who I was probably going to let go at the end of the season because I did not think he had a future at the club. Simon wanted me to play him in a central midfield role in the first team. I could not understand the logic of this 'request' because Will was not playing regularly for the reserves. Even so, Simon wanted him playing regularly in the middle of the park.

As far as I was concerned he didn't have the technical ability to play there and when I told Simon, he replied, 'Well, my father thinks he does!'

So I played him in the middle of the park. It was no surprise to me that he did not succeed in this role and he went on to make only four first team substitute appearances during his two-year period with the club, from 2002 to 2004.

This failure did not stop Simon accepting his father's opinion.

On another occasion I was told by Simon to give a first-team outing to a young defender called David. Hunt was his surname, I think. The game was at Selhurst Park against Wimbledon and we were about to defend a corner. The young lad was positioned on the near post and as the ball came towards him, he went to head it clear but mistimed his header and headed it into the back of our net. We lost the game 0-1 and not surprisingly the crowd were immediately hostile to me. This was not helpful because at the time I was going through a period when we were struggling to get consistent results. As a manager there can be no excuses. When the team is winning you take the praise but when results are not going well you are the fall guy. Hopefully these two examples illustrate how team selection is not always the sole responsibility of the manager!

Simon wanted me to prepare a blueprint for the forthcoming season, which I did. His request came at around Easter time so he was expecting me to be visionary, wanting answers to questions such as where would we be in the league after the first month?

How could I realistically answer that as I didn't know who we would be playing against, what my starting line-up would be and whether my top goalscorer would be available.

Even though I did not have the answers to these questions he insisted on this scientific approach. I tried to explain that football isn't as simple as that but he wanted it in writing so eventually I gave him the best I could under the circumstances.

Not surprisingly, he said it wasn't good enough and that I should take it away and do it again. I did it again and after looking at it for a couple of days he said there wasn't enough detail; he needed more meat on the bone! I was made to go away and do it again. I felt belittled – this was my fourth club as manager, a period totalling 12 years, and I felt as if I was being undermined. I questioned whether he was trying to box me into a corner with the obvious resultant repercussions.

A meeting was called when Simon was going to review my blueprint after I had tried to put more meat on the bone, as he wanted. Still I found it difficult because I did not have all the answers I needed for the following season. Of course I wanted the team to do better but it was dependent on so many things. I brought with me my two assistants, Terry Bullivant and Steve Kember, and informed them of what the crux of the meeting was about.

'I am telling you that this could all end tonight,' I said. I thought it only fair to explain the situation in which I found myself. They were anxious to know what I meant so I told them in no uncertain terms: 'I am not taking any shit.'

Before the meeting Terry and Steve said I should be careful about what I say because Simon could be volatile and could make a rash decision. Then I said I appreciated what they were saying but that they should be prepared for the worst. 'What do you mean?' was their response. I said, 'I am not going into the meeting and accepting any old shit. If he says something that I don't like then I'm not going to back down and will say exactly what I feel and I will accept the consequences. So be prepared.'

Not surprisingly that's exactly how it developed. During the meeting Simon got to me when we started talking about the blueprint. I said, 'Simon, listen, you seem to know all the answers so why don't you fucking manage the team?'

His response was that there was no point in continuing and he would see me tomorrow.

The following day it was training as normal in preparation for the next game and Simon wanted to meet me when training ended.

He opened the meeting by saying, 'Trev, I like you very much, and your family, but I can't have what happened last night.'

'Not a problem,' I replied, as I was treating this whole episode in a very matter of fact and philosophical way.

He said, 'That's fine. That's it as far as I am concerned. I will tell you now that if you do it right by me, and you don't go to the press and slag me off, I will look after you financially.'

I think I surprised him by saying, 'Simon, I would never consider going to the media. Thank you for giving me the opportunity to manage the club. I think it's the best outcome for the two of us.' He paid me up in full. I left on 19 April 2003.

Another of those myths which have followed me during my career is that Simon took delight in sacking me on my birthday. That was not the case and therefore another myth is dismissed.

I still see Simon Jordan now and then, because he stills spends time over in Marbella, and whenever our paths cross our relationship is very cordial. This is because I have the ability to differentiate between business and pleasure. I recall that when there were difficult financial restraints at the club, on at least two occasions the company credit card was declined when we tried to check into a hotel on a Friday night before a game. Both times, to avoid any embarrassment to the club or the players, I paid with my own credit card. One was close to home, at the Hilton hotel in Bromsgrove, prior to playing West Bromwich Albion. Obviously I was reimbursed and we still remain friends, but with a different attitude I could have caused problems for my employers.

I came out of Crystal Palace at the age of 49 and I felt I had had a tough time there. Whilst you can never say never in football, as I came away from Selhurst Park I was reviewing my employment status. Within minutes of my leaving I was thinking to myself that this was probably the end of my time in management. I was proved right. It would have been good to have stayed active in football management until I was 50 but it was not meant to be.

Hopefully the end of this chapter has surprised some of the readers. I guess that most people reading the book would expect me to be hammering Simon because of the way our relationship was depicted by the media. I am not interested in meeting the expectations of the media because I saw the private side of a man who projects to the outside world an entirely different personality of himself compared to the real Simon Jordan.

Chapter Thirteen

Reflections

INJURIES

When I reflect on all my career highlights I know I have given a lot of pleasure to the football supporters of every club for which I've played. I know this because I am always welcomed back with open arms because they enjoyed watching me as a footballer.

My only disappointment is that my football career was littered with injuries. Undoubtedly they handicapped me throughout the time I played but it was still a long career for which I am forever grateful. Even though I played for as long as I did, I know that I should have clocked up many more appearances. It is not just being out with an injury, it's trying to get yourself back to full fitness and then having to pick up the rhythm of where you left off. To have to do that once is bad enough but I had to do it on numerous occasions. Getting back to the level you want to perform at isn't that easy; it means long hours alone in the gym and with the medical team.

I enjoyed being at every club I joined and giving the fans pleasure, and I hope they enjoyed having me there, doing my thing. But I know it should have been so much better and I think my injuries prevented me from being a better player. I honestly believe that, even though I know many of my peers envy my playing record. But that's the way I feel.

I don't like the term 'injury-prone', but I wouldn't dispute it too much if students of the game (analysts) wanted to label me in that way. The annoying thing was that I looked after myself; even before I went to Italy I used to be careful with what I ate, what I drank. I consider myself to have been a good professional who trained hard but was very, very susceptible to muscle injuries. That was probably down to my 'speed off the mark' – not just the speed off the mark but also my quick, unusual movements. My muscles were not always up for it!

People ask me, are you bitter about the money the players are earning now? Absolutely not, but what I am envious of is the attention to detail that goes into the preparation to help footballers these days.

I'm not just talking about the quality of the playing surfaces, the quality of the footwear and the lightness of the ball, but about the science available now that shows that if you are fatigued you risk muscular injury – that would have benefitted me enormously. The dieticians at football clubs now are assisting footballers. That would have helped, but not as much as having the information that I was in the 'red zone' which would have told me that I was risking injury.

I can imagine myself playing now and the coach knowing that, as a player dependent on pace, I would need to be careful with any tiredness concerns. Today it might have meant being rested for one or two games, which would undoubtedly have helped me play more often. At Nottingham Forest we would often play midweek games and could have three games in the space of seven days. We would go over to Abu Dhabi and Bahrain for friendly games and I would go carrying an Achilles problem. So rather than resting, to help my Achilles recover, I continued playing. Clearly I had a problem because ultimately it snapped. I was required to play because the club had a lucrative deal which guaranteed I would play! It was made worse because I was having to play on rock-hard pitches in the Middle East. This undoubtedly led to my Achilles snapping.

THE PREMIER LEAGUE

The Premier League was when football started. Didn't you know that it wasn't until Sky Sports got involved that football began? I say that tongue in cheek but that's the way it feels sometimes.

ASSISTS

I never, ever considered myself to be an out-and-out goalscorer. Often I see my name in the statistical records, measured against my peer group on the basis of how many goals I scored in my career and my goals to games ratio.

As a forward I'm not suggesting I didn't love scoring goals but I have always felt that I was more of an all-round player.

In today's stats there is a focus on 'assists' which started in America. In the 1978/79 season assists were a big thing over there and it now seems to be bigger in England. I considered myself to be a good passer of the ball and certainly one of the best crosses of a ball there was, and I was able to cross a ball running at pace to the byline. Not many players can do that; scoring goals wasn't the be all and end all for me.

WASTED TALENT

Without a doubt George Best was the greatest player I played against in Britain and I was honoured to be asked to play in his testimonial in Belfast, Northern Ireland on 8 August 1988.

At the time Helen and I were living in a large thatched house on the Wentworth Estate. There had been a burglary at a house nearby and the police visited our house to check that everything was as it should be. The police remarked on the fact that Helen and the boys were alone and enquired about the whereabouts of her husband. She told them I was away in Ireland to which one of them said, 'Is he in the Army?' She replied, 'If he was he would need to be a sergeant major to have a house like this one!'

The game was played at Windsor Park between a Best XI and an International XI and featured players such as Ossie Ardiles, Paul Breitner, Wolfgang Overath, Johan Neeskens, Rudi Krol, Pat Jennings, Liam Brady and Johnny Rep. George's team won 7-6 although the result was immaterial.

I played against George on both sides of the Atlantic, in the United States for Detroit Express when he was playing with Fort Lauderdale, and in England for Birmingham City against Manchester United.

It was incredibly sad that his career was negatively impacted by his drink problem which, of course, was the ultimate cause of his death.

That self-damage is apparent with Paul Gascoigne. In 1988, in one of my early games for Queens Park Rangers, we travelled to St James' Park to play Newcastle United. In their team was a 21-year-old Gazza and I have never seen such a young footballer playing with such wonderful technical ability and confidence. He had great balance and outstanding dribbling ability, enabling him to beat players with ease. I realised I was watching a young player who was destined to be one of the best! On the long coach trip back to London I was talking to Jim Smith. We were eulogising about what we had seen and I said Gascoigne was the best I had seen since George Best.

This was another example of the game being robbed of a great talent too early. At least both players had incredible careers but all too short.

TODAY'S GAME

A question I am often asked is would I like to play football today. The answer is 'Yes' but not because of the money. There are so many advantages now for the modern footballer – the challenge from behind has gone, which makes life so much easier for a player with footballing skills. In my day the first challenge was down the back of the legs. Once the first centre-half had 'cleaned you out' the other centre-half would take his turn. It's good that tackling has been controlled but the quality of the pitches is the biggest difference. Forget all the diets and the scientific approach, which are obviously a huge help; the biggest bonus is the quality of the pitches. I couldn't even estimate the number of times a goalscoring opportunity was lost because of the pitch. A ball came over, you'd go to side-foot it into the back of the net and it would take a bobble, hit your shin and go over the crossbar or something. Some of the conditions we played in were atrocious mud baths. Also the lightness of the ball is a factor. I was regularly striking the old leather ball from 25–30 yards. If I was using today's ball I'd be able to strike it from the halfway line.

STRIKE PARTNERS

Throughout my career I was lucky enough to play with some wonderful partners up front.

There are many types of striker with various individual styles but all those I partnered had one key attribute – their excellent technical ability.

Despite my nine years at Birmingham City being a period when we never won anything I still look back with great fondness and realise how fortunate I was to play with three great strikers.

They were Bob Latchford, Peter Withe and Kenny Burns – all three strong physically but with plenty of skill on the ball and exceptional headers of the ball.

During my time at Nottingham Forest I played with Gary Birtles and Tony Woodcock on various occasions. Whilst not having the physical attributes of those I played with at Birmingham both had good technique, were good in the air and had fantastic pace. Both will go down in history for their great contributions to the club.

Talking of players that greatly contributed to the history of Forest, Roberto Mancini and Gianluca Vialli did likewise for Sampdoria.

During my season at Maine Road I played up front with Kevin Reeves, who was a hard-working striker with excellent qualities. It should be remembered that he was capped twice for England.

On the international front I was grateful to play with the talented Paul Mariner on 18 occasions. In all five matches in the 1982 World Cup I played alongside Paul. In the opening game he scored his only goal of the tournament against France whilst I got goals against Czechoslovakia and Kuwait. Our goals helped the team win all three matches. Despite our best efforts, the team could not score against Germany and Spain which resulted in us being eliminated from the World Cup. When football followers are discussing the merits of England teams over the years and in particular attacking players, Paul Mariner for some reason seems to be overlooked. He had an international career from 1977 through to 1985, winning 35 caps and scoring 13 goals. He was six feet tall, very mobile and was always an aerial threat.

Developing a strike partnership does not solely happen on the training ground, it takes time to evolve and improves for as long as the partnership lasts.

AUSTRALIA

After joining Queens Park Rangers in the March I played a handful of games. The English season had ended when I was offered the opportunity to be a guest player in Australia.

Two weeks was the length of my stay, which was more like a holiday for Helen, Matthew and me. Everything was on my terms. I refused to stay in Wollongong which was an hour and a half from Sydney, so we stayed in Sydney itself. I was 34 years of age and knew my fitness levels were good enough to fulfil my contract so I trained alone rather than making the three-hour round trip to Wollongong to train with the team. It reunited me with Alan Brazil, who I had played with at Detroit Express.

Designated a guest player, I was brought into Wollongong by a local television entrepreneur called Harry Michaels, who effectively paid for me to play three games as his team were looking to win a minor league championship. Hopefully my two goals helped. Two of the games were at home and the other was in Melbourne, where I scored the winner with the last kick of the game.

Harry also brought to Wollongong Paul Mariner of Ipswich Town fame, my England strike partner in the 1982 World Cup. But he was not there during the time I was in Australia.

Alan credits me with giving him the opportunity to play in Switzerland in the latter part of his career. I gave his telephone number to an ex-Forest team-mate of mine, Raimondo Ponte, who was setting up a team in Zurich which was to be called FC Baden. Raimondo followed up on my introduction which led to Alan playing six games during season 1988/89.

DISCIPLINARY MATTERS

During my career I have only received two yellow cards and been sent off once. This is a record of which I am not particularly proud.

My second yellow card was issued for feigning injury in the opinion of the referee, Norman Burtenshaw.

Note: In Burtenshaw's 1973 book, *Whose Side Are You On Ref*, he writes:

> One of the first players to be cautioned for pretending
> to be injured when he wasn't was the Birmingham City
> forward Trevor Francis. He was the first one I booked

for the offence. The match was Sheffield United v Birmingham City in February 1973. It was a pretty vital first division relegation game. There had been one or two incidents and I sent Bob Hatton of Birmingham off for striking an opponent whilst on the ground.

"There is no better player in the country than Trevor Francis."

Sir Alf Ramsey

I was bending over them trying to break it up and his right-hander nearly hit me! Later, I saw Francis suddenly fall down. The nearest Sheffield player said, 'I never touched him, ref'. I told him I could see that. I went to Francis and said, 'I am booking you for feigning injury. You could have got that other player sent off if I hadn't been looking.' Francis – who had a brilliant game, incidentally – said he didn't agree. I said, 'Well, are you injured? Do you want the trainer?' He replied that he didn't want the trainer. That incensed me. I found it hard to believe that a professional footballer would try to get a colleague sent off the field by such a deceitful trick. When I left Bramall Lane later that evening I was expecting to be asked by the press whether Francis had been booked. Unfortunately no one asked me; I hoped that some publicity about an aspect of the game the public knew very little about might contribute towards getting the practice of feigning injury stopped. Francis never appealed his caution.

NEPOTISM

Throughout my career I have come across the dreaded nepotism. I say dreaded because whilst the idea of a son inheriting the skills of his father is fine, the implications become difficult.

Ken Furphy is best known for his seven-year managerial stay at Watford which ended in 1971. He moved to America in 1976 after managing both Blackburn Rovers and Sheffield United for periods of two years. He managed Detroit Express for three years from 1977–80, which obviously included my time in the States. In his first year as manager he brought his son Keith into the squad. Now, let's be fair: in American terms Keith had a decent career stretching over 15 years whilst making over 450 appearances and scoring more than 250 goals. His talent meant nothing, though, because whenever Keith was selected to play, the reaction from the other players was, 'Why is he in the team?'

When I was at Manchester City there was a similar situation with John Bond and his son Kevin who also generated negative comments from his team-mates when selected for the first team.

Steve Bruce, who I signed for Birmingham City, helped the career of his son, Alex, on a number of occasions.

Naturally, I feel that a father should do everything he can to help his son in whatever career that might be, but with regards to football, being the manager of your son is difficult for both parties. When Bruce was a player at Manchester United his son was in their youth programme until he was released as a 16-year-old. Alex then signed for Birmingham City in January 2005 and after making a few Premier League appearances it was felt that accusations of nepotism were hindering his progress. It was decided that in the best interests of club, manager and player Bruce junior should pursue his career away from his father's management. Having said that, seven years later Steve signed Alex when he was managing Hull City.

As a young nine-year-old boy Nigel Clough was often seen carrying his father's overnight bag on to the team coach.

Later, as we know, Nigel went on to play for Forest under his father's management where he was known as 'my number 9' by his father.

No one would ever consider criticising Brian so when his son was selected to play for the first team there was never any negative comment.

As it happened Nigel was a good enough player to hold his own in any team, which is evidenced by the fact that he went on to play for England 14 times in the 1990s.

I have two sons who both showed talent at an early age but I would never have put them in the situation experienced by Keith Furphy, Alex Bruce and Kevin Bond.

When working for your father you need to be incredibly talented and to make a big difference to the team and its performances.

ROYAL SHAKESPEARE THEATRE

This greeting card is stocked in the shop of the Royal Shakespeare Company theatre in Stratford-upon-Avon.

In my introduction I state that I am not interested in what people say about me but I make an exception for anyone who is a knight of the realm.

It retails at £3 and, whilst the image is not a great one of me, the inscription says it all: 'There is no better player in the country than Trevor Francis. Sir Alf Ramsey.' He said this when he was managing Birmingham City during the period 1977–78.

Chapter Fourteen

2003 to 2018

I LEFT Crystal Palace in 2003 and still people often ask, 'Are you still involved in football?'

It is a fair question, as football has been part of my life since I became involved in the game as a schoolboy player at the age of seven. My playing career ended some 32 years later when I left Sheffield Wednesday.

The transition to my becoming a manager coincided with my being approached by Sky Sports to see if I was interested in a part-time career in the media.

My reply was in the affirmative and an involvement of 21 years followed.

What made me say 'Yes' to Sky Sports? Well, I have been lucky throughout my life to have had jobs or roles that I find enjoyable and it seemed to me that media work could also be interesting, fun and therefore enjoyable, and involve working with people who had a very professional attitude to their jobs.

My footballing career also gave me the opportunity to travel the world and I saw working for Sky Sports as another chance to visit foreign countries. For example, in 1996 as part of the Sky Sports team I was in Hong Kong and China covering the England international team.

I remember walking along the Great Wall of China with Alan Shearer getting an insight into his thoughts on his ex-colleague at Blackburn Rovers, Mike Newell, who I was considering being one of my early signings at Birmingham City.

It transpired that the Sky Sports deal, which was an exclusive one – i.e., I was not allowed to work for any other media company – meant that I began co-commentating on their Monday night games and England games.

Surprisingly, I did not receive any media training (I suppose you can draw parallels with the first ten years of my footballing career when I did not receive any specialised coaching) and therefore learnt on the job, getting help from my commentator colleagues.

The match routine was also uncomplicated. I had to get to the game two hours before kick-off. Over a period of time commentators build up such a relationship with the managers that they often get access to the team sheet before the opposition. This was a clear demonstration of the confidence shown by the managers in the commentators that confidentiality would be upheld.

Once we had the team sheet we had a pretty good idea as to the shape of the team and how they were going to play. This meant that the remaining time before the start of the match was spent preparing for the game. For example, since the influx of foreign players into the English game, the pronunciation of first names and surnames has become a growing issue for commentators and pundits alike. I was always briefed well before the game and spent time rehearsing how to say certain names. This has become easier since the introduction of press officers in recent times, whose role is to brief and help media personnel.

My time with Sky Sports ended four years ago in 2014 which meant I had effectively been with them since the formation of the Premier League.

However, sometimes you just can't win. In January 2017 I was co-commentating when working for BT Sport on Liverpool against Swansea and James Milner was having a good game. Because of this I said that I would like to see Milner back in an England shirt. I got criticism all over social media because he had retired from international football on 11 June 2016. The impression was given that I had got the facts wrong but that was way off the mark as I knew he had retired. But on the evidence of his performance in that match I felt he had retired far too soon and I would have liked to have seen the England team manager, Gareth Southgate, who had a shortage of quality midfield players at his disposal, maybe look to have a word with James Milner to get him to reconsider his position.

As a co-commentator there are certain things that you very quickly pick up as you go along. I always tried to be honest with my comments and tell it as I saw it. But it becomes difficult, of course, when you are criticising players whilst you are still very much involved in the game. Clearly it is a lot easier when you are outside the industry.

One thing I was told by my bosses in my early days was that when doing a commentary it is absolutely essential that you don't talk over a goal. This is the role of the commentator – this is a golden rule. When there is any chance of a goal the pundit has to shut up!

In Italy this is not a problem due to the slower pace of the game but in the English game it is much more difficult as the flow of the game can change so rapidly.

After Sky Sports I had a two-year stint with BT Sport, which was not an exclusive deal and which finished in 2017. Under the terms of the BT Sport agreement I was able to work with other media companies and over the past eight years I have travelled to Doha, the capital city of Qatar, to do television work for Al Jazeera which has recently been rebranded as beIN Sports.

In recent years I have come into contact with my ex-Sky Sports mates Richard Keys and Andy Gray, who now live permanently in Qatar.

Football followers in the Middle East are benefitting from their television expertise which in my opinion has been sorely missed by English viewers.

I consider myself to be privileged to have experienced the incredible growth of Doha during those eight years.

Naturally I have shown great interest in how the stadiums are being built in preparation for the 2022 World Cup.

Like many people I was pleasantly surprised by how successful the 2018 World Cup was in Russia. It is my expectation that the Qatar competition will be even better than Russia. Why? Well, finances are not a problem and the stadiums will be quite fantastic.

There will be a major benefit for the travelling fans moving from venue to venue for games: Qatar is relatively small and therefore it will be very easy to get from A to B.

At the time of writing this book I was still hearing reports about how ridiculous it will be playing football in the high temperatures likely in Qatar. I can tell you that this is nonsense, because the games will be played in November and December – their winter – when temperatures will not be a problem. They will be perfect.

I have one major business interest – Francis Homes which I run with my sons Matthew and James. How do I describe what I do? Well, that's best left to what is on our website:

Francis Homes are a Midlands based premium homebuilder, dedicated to building exceptional homes for modern, contemporary living. We have strong and long-standing relationships with our contractors and craftsmen, all driven to developing exclusive, unique living spaces in sought after locations.

We focus on the south side of Birmingham and our first development is called 'Helen's Gate' in honour of my late wife.

What else do I do? I do quite a lot of corporate work, attending events/dinners to take part in question and answer sessions.

I also do meet and greet work for the Football Association in the Bobby Moore Suite at Wembley, along with other ex-England internationals.

The biggest challenge recently has been the rebuilding of my life since Helen sadly passed away in April 2017. We were married in 1974 and were inseparable throughout our marriage. As you will know from reading this book she has been alongside me throughout my career. Life without her is so difficult.

Appendix
England Career And Goals

MY time as an England Youth international was highly successful, not only for me but for the country as well.

I was involved in two 'Little World Cup' tournaments, the first in 1971 in Czechoslovakia and the second a year later in Spain. Although known as the Little World Cup, the event's formal title was the UEFA European Under-18 Championships.

CZECHOSLOVAKIA

In 1971 I was nominated as 'Best Player'.

As one of eight teams that entered the competition without playing any qualification games we went straight into Group D alongside Yugoslavia, Poland and Sweden.

Our games were:

22 May 1971 v Yugoslavia Youth – won 1-0
24 May 1971 v Sweden Youth – won 1-0

26 May 1971 v Poland Youth – drew 0-0

We played the Soviet Union in Prague in the semi-final and got through 4-2 on penalties after drawing 1-1 after extra time.

We beat Portugal 3-0 in the final on 30 May. The team was: Tilsed – Dugdale – Dillon – Parker – Shanks – McGuire – Busby – Ayris – Francis – Eastoe – Daley.

This was England's fourth title. Bill Shorthouse was our manager.

SPAIN

In Spain we won Group C which also contained the Republic of Ireland, Belgium and Yugoslavia.

Our games were:

13 May 1972 v Belgium – drew 0-0
15 May 1972 v Republic of Ireland – won 4-0
17 May 1972 v Yugoslavia – won 1-0

With five points from our group games we were drawn against Poland in the semi-final on 20 May in Valencia. A 1-0 victory meant an appearance in the final two days later in Barcelona, against arch rivals West Germany. We won 2-0. Gordon Milne was the part-time manager who took England to their fifth title. The youth set-up was a great experience and served me well as I progressed to play five times for the England Under-23 team.

10 October 1973 England 0 Poland 0

Home Park, Plymouth. 18,230

Team: Latchford P. – McDowell – Sullivan – Cantello – Taylor – Beattie – Francis – Perryman – Johnson – Kennedy (Richards) – George.

13 November 1973 England 1 (R. Latchford) Denmark 1 (Pettersen)

Fratton Park, Portsmouth. 18,611

Team: Stevenson – McDowell – Sullivan – Cantello – Taylor – Maddren – Francis T. – Perryman (Thomas) – Latchford R. – Francis G. – George (Fletcher).

16 January 1974 England 0 Wales 0

Ashton Gate, Bristol. 3,117

Team: Latchford P. – Palmer – Mills – McDermott – Taylor – Beattie – Francis – Fletcher – Latchford R. – Richards – Perryman.

18 November 1975 England 2 (Taylor P. and Mills) Portugal 0

Selhurst Park. 19,472

Team: Day – Gidman – Kennedy – Towers – Taylor T. – Dodd – Wilkins – Francis (Mills) – Johnson – Taylor P. – Armstrong.

10 March 1976 Under-23 European Championships quarter-final Hungary 3 (Nyilasi (2), Szabo) England 0

Nepstadion, Budapest. 22,000

One in a Million

Team: Wallington – Gidman – Kennedy – Towers – Thompson – Dodd – Francis T. (Mills) – Johnson – Greenhoff – Hudson – Francis G.

My full international England career is detailed in the table opposite:

Number	Manager	Match	Date	Competition	Result	Notes
1	Don Revie	Netherlands	9 February 1977	Friendly	0-2	
2	Don Revie	Luxembourg	30 March 1977	Friendly	5-0	Scored
3	Don Revie	Scotland	4 June 1977	Home Championship	1-2	
4	Don Revie	Brazil	8 June 1977	Friendly	0-0	
5	Ron Greenwood	Switzerland	7 September 1977	Friendly	0-0	
6	Ron Greenwood	Luxembourg	12 October 1977	World Cup Qualifier	2-0	
7	Ron Greenwood	Italy	16 November 1977	World Cup Qualifier	2-0	Came on as substitute
8	Ron Greenwood	West Germany	22 February 1978	Friendly	1-2	Came on as substitute
9	Ron Greenwood	Brazil	19 April 1978	Friendly	1-1	
10	Ron Greenwood	Wales	13 May 1978	Home Championship	3-1	
11	Ron Greenwood	Scotland	20 May 1978	Home Championship	1-0	
12	Ron Greenwood	Hungary	24 May 1978	Friendly	4-1	Scored

Number	Manager	Match	Date	Competition	Result	Notes
13	Ron Greenwood	Bulgaria	6 June 1979	European Championship Qualifier	3-0	Came on as substitute
14	Ron Greenwood	Sweden	10 June 1979	Friendly	0-0	
15	Ron Greenwood	Austria	13 June 1979	Friendly	3-4	Came on as substitute
16	Ron Greenwood	Northern Ireland	17 October 1979	European Championship Qualifier	5-1	Scored twice
17	Ron Greenwood	Bulgaria	22 November 1979	European Championship Qualifier	2-0	
18	Ron Greenwood	Spain	26 March 1980	Friendly	2-0	Scored and substituted
19	Ron Greenwood	Spain	25 March 1981	Friendly	1-2	Substituted
20	Ron Greenwood	Romania	29 April 1981	World Cup Qualifier	0-0	
21	Ron Greenwood	Scotland	23 May 1981	Home Championship	0-1	Came on as substitute

Number	Manager	Match	Date	Competition	Result	Notes
22	Ron Greenwood	Switzerland	30 May 1981	World Cup Qualifier	1-2	Substituted
23	Ron Greenwood	Norway	9 September 1981	World Cup Qualifier	1-2	
24	Ron Greenwood	Northern Ireland	23 February 1982	Home Championship	4-0	Substituted
25	Ron Greenwood	Wales	27 April 1982	Home Championship	1-0	Scored and substituted
26	Ron Greenwood	Scotland	29 May 1982	Home Championship	1-0	Came on as substitute
27	Ron Greenwood	Finland	3 June 1982	Friendly	4-1	Came on as substitute
28	Ron Greenwood	France	16 June 1982	World Cup Finals	3-1	
29	Ron Greenwood	Czechoslovakia	20 June 1982	World Cup Finals	2-0	Scored
30	Ron Greenwood	Kuwait	25 June 1982	World Cup Finals	1-0	Scored

Number	Manager	Match	Date	Competition	Result	Notes
31	Ron Greenwood	West Germany	29 June 1982	World Cup Finals	0-0	Substituted
32	Ron Greenwood	Spain	5 July 1982	World Cup Finals	0-0	
33	Bobby Robson	Denmark	22 September 1982	European Championship Qualifier	2-2	Scored twice
34	Bobby Robson	Greece	30 March 1983	European Championship Qualifier	0-0	
35	Bobby Robson	Hungary	27 April 1983	European Championship Qualifier	2-0	Scored
36	Bobby Robson	Northern Ireland	28 May 1983	Home Championship	0-0	
37	Bobby Robson	Scotland	1 June 1983	Home Championship	2-0	

Number	Manager	Match	Date	Competition	Result	Notes
38	Bobby Robson	Australia	12 June 1983	Friendly	0-0	
39	Bobby Robson	Australia	15 June 1983	Friendly	1-0	
40	Bobby Robson	Australia	19 June 1983	Friendly	1-1	Scored and yellow card
41	Bobby Robson	Denmark	21 September 1983	European Championship Qualifier	0-1	
42	Bobby Robson	Northern Ireland	4 April 1984	Home Championship	1-0	
43	Bobby Robson	Russia	2 June 1984	Friendly	0-2	Substituted
44	Bobby Robson	East Germany	19 September 1984	Friendly	1-0	Came on as substitute
45	Bobby Robson	Turkey	14 November 1984	World Cup Qualifier	8-0	Came on as substitute
46	Bobby Robson	Northern Ireland	27 February 1985	World Cup Qualifier	1-0	Came on as substitute
47	Bobby Robson	Romania	1 May 1985	World Cup Qualifier	0-0	

Number	Manager	Match	Date	Competition	Result	Notes
48	Bobby Robson	Finland	22 May 1985	World Cup Qualifier	1-1	
49	Bobby Robson	Scotland	25 May 1985	Rous Cup	0-1	
50	Bobby Robson	Italy	6 June 1985	Ciudad de Mexico Cup	1-2	Substituted
51	Bobby Robson	Mexico	9 June 1985	Ciudad de Mexico Cup	0-1	
52	Bobby Robson	Scotland	23 April 1986	Rous Cup	2-1	

I made 42 starts and ten substitute appearances and was withdrawn on eight occasions, bringing my total number of full games to 34.

Bibliography

Tony Matthews, *Birmingham City – The Complete Record* (DB Publishing, 2010).

Ian King, *Crystal Palace – The Complete Record 1905-2011* (DB Publishing, 2011).

John Brodie and Jason Dickinson, *Sheffield Wednesday – The Complete Record 1867-2011* (DB Publishing, 2011).

Bob Ferrier and Robert McElroy, *Rangers – The Complete Record* (Breedon Books Publishing, 2005).

Gary James, *Manchester City – The Complete Record* (DB Publishing, 2010).

Norman Burtenshaw, *Whose Side Are You On, Ref?* (Arthur Barker Limited, 1973).

Pete Attaway, *Nottingham Forest – A Complete Record 1865–1991* (Breedon Books Sport, 1991).

Don Wright, *Forever Forest – The Official 150th Anniversary History of the Original Reds* (Amberley, 2015).

Gordon Macey, *Queens Park Rangers – The Complete Record 1899–2009* (DB Publishing, 2009).

David Clayton, *Everything Under the Blue Moon* (Mainstream Publishing, 2001).

Jason Dickinson, *Sheffield Wednesday – The Official History 1867–2017* (Amberley, 2017).

Kenny Burns, *No ifs or butts* (Kenny Burns Promotions, November 2009).

Index